מסורה

ArtScroll Series®

Rabbi Nosson Scherman / Rabbi Meir Zlotowitz

General Editors

LIVING &

Published by

Mesorah Publications, ltd

PARENTING

A Down-to-Earth Guide

FIRST EDITION
First Impression … March 2008

Published and Distributed by
MESORAH PUBLICATIONS, LTD.
4401 Second Avenue / Brooklyn, N.Y 11232

Distributed in Europe by
LEHMANNS
Unit E, Viking Business Park
Rolling Mill Road
Jarow, Tyne & Wear, NE32 3DP
England

Distributed in Australia and New Zealand by
GOLDS WORLDS OF JUDAICA
313- William Street
Balaclava, Melbourne 3183
Victoria, Australia

Distributed in Israel by
SIFRIATI / A. GITLER — BOOKS
6 Hayarkon Street
Bnei Brak 51127

Distributed in South Africa by
KOLLEL BOOKSHOP
Ivy Common
105 William Road
Norwood 2192, Johannesburg, South Africa

ISBN 10: 12-0642-4226- / ISBN 13: 9781-0642-4226-1- (hard cover)
ISBN 10: 10-0643-4226- / ISBN 13: 9788-0643-4226-1- (paperback)

Typography by CompuScribe at ArtScroll Studios, Ltd.
Printed in the United States of America by Noble Book Press Corp.
Bound by Sefercraft, Quality Bookbinders, Ltd., Brooklyn N.Y. 11232

This book is dedicated in loving memory of our dear father,

REB SHLOME HOROWITZ ע״ה

לזכר נשמת

ר׳ שלמה בן ר׳ יעקב משה הלוי האראוויץ ע״ה

נפטר בשם טוב א׳ אייר תשכ״ג

Hashem, in His infinite wisdom, took you from this world
far too early for us to get to know you well.

However, over the years, we were introduced to you often —
through the eyes of the hundreds of your friends and family members
whose lives you touched so deeply.

Those eyes spoke volumes as they softened when describing your
outstanding middos tovos, your kindness, and your generosity of spirit.

We are so very proud of the sterling legacy that you left us,
and feel privileged to carry your name.

With everlasting love,

DVORA OSTREICHER   YAKOV HOROWITZ
YEHUDAH HOROWITZ

This book is dedicated in honor of our beloved parents

SHLOMO AND BEILE NUTOVIC לאי״ט

With love, patience, and wisdom, you were always there to guide us.
You encouraged each of us to chart our own course in life and to
pursue our dreams.

Children could ask for no more.

May the Ribbono Shel Olam grant us many, many more years
of your guidance, wisdom and love.

ISAAC AND SHIFRA NUTOVIC   CHAIM AND DVORA OSTREICHER
YAKOV AND UDI HOROWITZ   YEHUDAH AND ETTY HOROWITZ
VOLVIE AND CHANTZIE ROSENBERG

CONTENTS

ACKNOWLEDGMENTS

This book touches upon many complex parenting and *chinuch* issues. I consider myself fortunate to have received guidance and training in these areas from my great *rebbi*, **Rabbi Avrohom Yaakov Pam** *zt'l* and, *yibadlu l'chayim tovim,* the **Novominsker Rebbi, Rabbi Yaakov Perlow**, *s'hlita,* Rosh Agudas Yisroel, and **Rabbi Shmuel Kamenetsky** *s'hlita,* Rosh HaYeshivah of the Philadelphia Yeshivah, who has served as the rabbinic advisor of Project Y.E.S. since its inception. These Torah leaders all graciously took time from their busy schedules and made themselves available to patiently share their *da'as Torah* with me and with the staff members of Project Y.E.S. whenever called upon. I am forever in their debt.

Although I only had the *zechus* of working with him for slightly more than a year in the formative phase of Project Y.E.S., I will always consider **Rabbi Moshe Sherer** *z'tl* to be my *rebbi* in *askanus* (public service). His selfless devotion to the community, impeccable integrity, and keen insight were legendary and inspirational to all who had the privilege of knowing him. In the ten years since Rabbi Sherer's passing, **Rabbis Shmuel Bloom, Chaim Dovid Zwiebel**, and **Shlomo Gertzulin**, *yibadlu l'chayim tovim*, have shouldered the vast array of communal responsibilities that are part and parcel of Agudath Israel. I am grateful for their assistance to me personally and to Project Y.E.S. as a whole. I am also indebted to **Rabbi Labish Becker**, Associate Executive Director of Agudath Israel, for his active involvement in Project Y.E.S. over the years. May *Hashem* grant them the strength and wisdom to lead the Agudah and help *Klal Yisrael* for many years to come.

Our community owes an enormous debt of gratitude to the lay leaders who chaired Project Y.E.S. over the past eleven years: **Shiya Markowitz, Dovid Weldler, Leon Melohn**, and our current chairs, **Harry Skydell** and **Mark Karasik. Rabbi Avrohom Meir Gluck**, our Director of Operations, has been my partner in Project Y.E.S. since 1998 and brings professionalism and a high standard of quality to all our programs. As a grass-roots organization, Project Y.E.S. owes it success to the many hundreds of volunteers who — under the supervision of our mental health professionals, department heads, and interns — dedicate their personal time to mentoring children, teens, and their parents.

This book is being released in conjunction with the Eleventh Annual Dinner of Yeshivah Darchei Noam. These are exciting times at Darchei Noam, as we prepare to join with Yeshivah Ohr Reuvain under the leadership of **Rabbi Betzalel Rudinsky** *s'hlita* and continue the process of building a permanent home for our growing student body of 270 *talmidim, kein yirbu.* I would like to offer my boundless gratitude to our *Menahel*, **Rabbi Yonah G. Lazar** *s'hlita*, my partner in Yeshivah Darchei Noam for the past five years. I would also like to express my *hakoras hatov* to the department heads, rebbei'im and faculty members at Yeshivah Darchei Noam for all they do to create such an outstanding, nurturing environment for our *talmidim.* Darchei Noam is a child-centered yeshivah where every child really matters and where the *rebbei'im* and teachers are always looking to grow personally and professionally. I am honored to be part of an exciting *makom Torah* which has become an incubator for *chinuch* excellence and innovation.

A master *rebbi* is one who understands his *talmid* and inspires him. A master *rebbi* is one who cares enough to constructively criticize his *talmid* and encourage him toward self-realization. Most importantly, a master *rebbi* promotes the independence of his *talmid* and is bold enough to risk selflessly fading into the background in the face of his *talmid's* growth. I have been fortunate to gain from the wisdom and experience of the *"menahel's menahel"*: **Rabbi Chaim Feuerman**, *s'hlita*, a master *rebbi* in every sense of the word. I am forever grateful for his guidance and *hadrachah* in *chinuch* and personal matters over the years.

Since I began writing, I have had the privilege of working with the editors and support staff of the numerous periodicals in which the articles in this book originally appeared; **Rabbi Nisson Wolpin** of *The Jewish Observer,* **Mrs. Naomi Mauer** of *The Jewish Press,* **Mrs. Faige Safran** of *Mishpacha Family Magazine,* **Rabbi Pinchos Lipshitz** of *Yated Ne'eman,* and **Mrs. Ruth Lichtenstein** and **Mrs. Rochel Roth** of *Hamodia.*

The advent of email has opened new vistas for disseminating Torah thought and parenting advice. I would like to thank those responsible for setting up and maintaining the website email system used to disseminate my *divrei Torah* and parenting columns to our thousands of subscribers worldwide: **Rabbi Avrohom Meir Gluck, Reb Shlome Henig, Rabbi Tzvi Rosenblum, Mr. Yaakov Colman**, and **Mr. Effie Rosenberg**. I am also grateful to my dear chaverim **Shmuel (Sammy) Moeller** for loaning me a laptop of his in the winter of 1995-96 when I wrote my first column, and to my 'tech-rebbi' **Shragie Lieber**, for patiently tutoring me in computer and communication technology over the past six years.

Thirty years ago, when I was Gedaliah Zlotowitz's Junior Counselor, his father, **Rabbi Meir Zlotowitz**, gave me a generous tip and a copy of *Megillas Eichah*, the third *sefer* produced by ArtScroll/

Mesorah. That *sefer,* and the countless others that followed it, were welcomed by Torah Jews throughout the world with joy and appreciation. In the three decades since, the "ArtScroll Revolution" has disseminated Torah and Jewish values on a scale perhaps unparalleled in our glorious history, and has enabled all members of our community to access Torah wisdom. I am honored to join the illustrious ranks of ArtScroll authors and look forward to working with Rabbi Zlotowitz and **Rabbi Nosson Sherman** – with whom I have been fortunate to have developed a close, personal relationship – for many years to come.

I would like to extend my sincere thanks to the entire team at ArtScroll: **Mrs. Deborah Schechter's** sensitive reading and insightful comments were on the mark; **Reb Avrohom Biderman** partnered with me in the creation of this book; **Mendy Herzberg** deftly coordinated the production; **Nechama Nafisi** designed the striking and creative cover and page design; **Mrs. Faygie Weinbaum** and **Mrs. Frimy Eisner** proofread; **Mrs. Danit Gantz** coordinated with my staff on the corrections; and **Suri Reinhold** and **Devori Weissblum** entered the many editorial revisions. I thank **Rabbi Yaakov Winkler** for his perceptive remarks on a number of the chapters.

Over the years, I have been fortunate to have retained outstanding executive assistants to help manage my many responsibilities. I would like to offer my sincere appreciation and gratitude to **Mrs. Shaindy (Horowitz) Pam, Mrs. Esther (Gluck) Martin, Mrs. Esty (Krishevsky) Genuth,** and **Mrs. Chaya Becker** for their unruffled and professional assistance, and their help with the columns which were transformed into this book. Additionally, I would like to thank **Mr. Steve Mayer** for his friendship and support over the past six years.

This book is dedicated in loving memory of my dear father, **Reb Shlome Horowitz** *a'h,* who passed away suddenly in 1963 at the young age of 41, and, *yibodel l'chaim tovim,* in honor of my dear parents, **Shlomo and Beile Nutovic**. Please see the Afterword for more details and some family background.

To my parents, Shlomo and Beile Nutovic: thanks for your unwavering backing, support, and the "I-don't-care-how-old-you-are-I'm-still-your-parent" advice that I still enjoy and treasure so much. To my in-laws, **Leibel and Bracha Berger**: thanks for your encouragement, assistance — and for raising a one-in-a-million daughter. May *Hashem* grant Udi and me the *zechus* of your guidance for many years to come, and may we be *zocheh* to have you share in all our *simchos* in good health.

To our dear children: **Baruch, Shlomie & Kaila Horowitz, Leah & Moshe Webster, Faigy & Dovid Meir Loeb**, and, of course **Sara**; thank you for sharing me so graciously with the *klal* and for giving Mommy and me such unending *nachas* over the past twenty-six years.

I feel that of all the kindness that *Hashem* bestowed upon me in my lifetime, I am most grateful to Him for sending me my life-partner: my wife **Udi**. Throughout the past twenty-seven years, she has been my bedrock and support system; my sounding-board, confidant, best friend, and my full partner. She gives of herself selflessly and without any personal agenda. She is content to be left to raise our children and pursue her career and interests; but always drops everything and offers her incredible range of talents to help me realize my dreams. She is an outstanding mother to our children, and always steps in to fill any void when my responsibilities take me away from home.

Only *Hashem* can tally the countless thousands of hours that she has devoted since the founding of Project Y.E.S. to comfort, guide, and support broken-hearted and frightened parents of at-risk teens around the world. When the demands of my schedule do not permit me to take their phone calls or respond to their emails, they know that they can confidently turn to her for sound direction and encouragement — and they do. May He repay her with our greatest

Finally, and most importantly, I would like to humbly give thanks to *Hashem* for allowing me to "dwell in His House" (Tehillim 27:4) and to bring Torah to His children.

Yakov Horowitz
10 Adar II 5768
Monsey, N.Y.

INTRODUCTION

The first fifteen years of our married life were wonderful and tranquil ones. I taught eighth grade; first in Yeshivah Toras Emes in Brooklyn, and later in Yeshivah of Spring Valley in Monsey. I also held down a variety of afternoon and summer camp administrative jobs to help pay the bills of our growing family.

When I started teaching, the term "at-risk teen" had not joined the vernacular of the Torah world and there was little understanding regarding the educational and social needs of these kids. I still remember the advice given to me by a veteran educator when I informed him of my intention to volunteer for "riot duty" — teaching the weaker eighth grade in Yeshivah Toras Emes in 1982. Horrified at my naiveté, he tried to convince me to change my mind. "Yankie," he said, "You are in a no-win situation. If you are good [at teaching a weaker class], you will never get the opportunity to teach an 'alef' (advanced) class. And if you do not do well, you will get fired."

Ignoring his advice, I jumped into the frying pan — teaching a class of twenty-six underachieving eighth-graders at the age of twenty-two, with little in the way of experience or training. Well, I didn't get fired, and thoroughly enjoyed the challenging and rewarding job of teaching boys who had not yet succeeded in yeshivah.

I was, however, saddened beyond words at the despair that I kept seeing in the eyes and hearts of underachieving kids, and began devoting more of my free time to helping them. Word got out that a *charedi* rabbi was willing to work with at-risk adolescents, and during the first half of the 1990's, more and more teens and their parents approached me for assistance.

When I decided to write my first column, "An Ounce of Prevention," (p.33) in the winter of 1995–96, I honestly had no idea of the impact it would have and the firestorm it would ignite. But I soon discovered the incredible power of the written word. In the first month after the column was published in *The Jewish Observer*, my wife and I received more than 300 phone calls at home from parents around the corner and around the world. Some complimented or critiqued what I had written, but the vast majority of them were just begging for relief from the searing agony their at-risk children were experiencing. Clearly a raw nerve had been touched. Subsequently, I was invited to address the National Conventions of Torah Umesorah and Agudath Israel and speak at several parenting conferences on the issue of teens at risk. Over the following months, I wrote several follow-up columns on this topic ("A Pound of Cure," "Report From Ground Zero," and "Independent Counsel"), pages 47-69.

Then, one week after the *Siyum HaShas* in September of 1997, I faxed a memo to Rabbi Moshe Sherer, the late, dynamic President of Agudath Israel, requesting a meeting with him to explore the possibility of harnessing the resources of the Agudah to address the issue of at-risk teens. At that time, he was well past retirement age, and was silently battling the ravages of the illness that would take his life in the not-too-distant future. He must have been basking in the glow of the beautiful *Siyum Hashas* one week earlier, when he spoke to 70,000 Jews in 35 cities across the country on a video hookup, the first time this technology had been used for *k'vod Shamayim* on that scale. It would have been well within his right to take a two-week vacation and disconnect his phone. But his dedication to *Klal Yisrael* did not permit him to do so. He took the time that week to meet with me and was actively involved in the founding and growth of Project Y.E.S. over the following months – almost until the week of his *petirah*. (See "Basic Training," my tribute to Rabbi Sherer, p.245).

The past eleven years have seen great forward strides in our understanding and awareness of the teens-at-risk issue. We have demonstrated our willingness to create programs in our mainstream schools and outside of them to prevent kids from slipping — and to support them when they fall. However, we still have a long way to go, and now, with the advent of exponentially growing technology, new challenges face us in the months and years ahead. About two years ago, I began experiencing a sinking sensation of déjà vu as I kept seeing all around me signs of what I fear may be a second, potentially larger, wave of teens (and adults) at risk. As a result of this growing concern, in December 2006, I began writing an ongoing series of columns that appear in Mishpacha Family Magazine, some of which can be found in this book. (These columns appear in this book in a thematic not sequential order. The first column of the Mishpacha series appears on page 204. Other recent Mishpacha columns can be found in pages 70-87, 101-113, and 210-240)

I have always felt that awareness and education are the first critical steps in resolving problems of any sort. With this in mind, I feel that the columns that appear in this book are important ones to read, even if doing so may generate discomfort and perhaps unease.

Hopefully, the communal dialogue that emerges from discussions of the issues raised in these essays will help us realize our heartfelt and shared goal — that all our sons and daughters reach their fullest potential and transmit our *mesorah* to future generations of proud, committed Torah Jews.

Yakov Horowitz
10 Adar II 5768
Monsey, N.Y.

Chapter One

ANSWERS ABOUT QUESTIONS

A PRIMER ON SEEKING DA'AS TORAH

HADRACHAH — ABOUT *HADRACHAH*

*I*t is a wonderful expression of the Torah community's reverence for *Da'as Torah* that we consult with our *gedolim* and *rabbanim* before making significant decisions. I have found, though, that one of the areas where proper *hadrachah* (guidance) is most needed these days is in the area of getting proper *hadrachah*. There is a significant amount of confusion and misinformation about how to prepare for, frame, ask, and listen to guidance from a rav, *moreh* *derech* (guide), or *gadol*. And, in this increasingly complex world in which we live, getting proper *Da'as Torah* is more important that ever.

In my twenty-five years in *chinuch*, and much more so, in the nine years since Project Y.E.S. and Yeshiva Darchei Noam were founded, I have met with and spoken to hundreds of couples who have presented *chinuch* and parenting issues to their *rabbanim* and *roshei yeshivah*. From this vantage point, patterns emerge which suggest that certain pointers and adequate preparation can make the experience a more productive and fulfilling one. Hopefully, these lines will provide you, the reader, with suggestions that will help you seek the advice of our *gedolim* and *morei derech* in a manner that is helpful and productive.

I write these lines having had the privilege of spending a few precious months under the close tutelage of the great Rabbi Moshe Sherer *z'tl*, president of Agudath Israel, as Project Y.E.S. was founded during the sunset of his illustrious life. Rabbi Sherer patiently guided me as I consulted with *gedolim* and maneuvered through the many complex issues we faced where *Da'as Torah* was urgently needed.

I have also had the *zechus* to have the guidance and *Da'as Torah* of my great Rebbi, Rav Avrohom Pam *z'tl*, and, *yibodel l'chayim*, that of Rav Shmuel Kaminetsky *shlita*, who has served as the *moreh derech* for Project Y.E.S. for many years. Listening to their sage advice often reminded me of the words written about those who were present in the court of Shlomo Hamelech, ... אַשְׁרֵי אֲנָשֶׁיךָ הָעֹמְדִים לְפָנֶיךָ תָּמִיד הַשֹּׁמְעִים אֶת חָכְמָתֶיךָ — Fortunate are your men ... who stand before you constantly, who hear your wisdom (*I Kings* 10:8).

It is my humble wish that these lines will help you in your quest for that which we daven for each day in the Ma'ariv *tefillah*; וְתַקְּנֵנוּ בְּעֵצָה טוֹבָה מִלְּפָנֶיךָ — Set us right with good counsel from before You.

PREPARING TO ASK

*B*efore going to a *gadol*, ask yourself: which of the following am I seeking: a *berachah* (blessing), a *p'sak* (halachic ruling) or an *eitzah* (advice)?

A **berachah** is a request for an *adam gadol* to wish you success in whatever you have already made up your mind to do.

Looking for a **p'sak** means ascertaining what the halachah requires you to do in a particular instance.

Seeking an **eitzah** is a highly personalized request for guidance; a very complex procedure. This will be the main focus of this article.

GETTING A *BERACHAH*

*S*eeking a *berachah* is a rather straightforward procedure. You set a time to visit the *gadol*, and inform him what you are about to do: (I am starting a business venture; my daughter is about to become a *kallah*; we decided to make *aliyah*). You then ask the *gadol* for a *berachah*, and upon receiving one, you feel comforted that you have the *zechus* to have a *gadol* bless your actions.

SEEKING AN *EITZAH*

*T*he quest for an *eitzah* is an entirely different matter. In this case, you are asking a *gadol* to advise you which course of action to take when you have two or more halachically and morally permissible options. (If you are questioning the halachic appropriateness of your options, you are seeking a *p'sak* — a very different matter entirely.)

If it is an *eitzah* you are looking for, there are many issues that need to be clarified before you go to a *gadol* to seek his advice:

Do I really know what I want — am I properly prepared to ask for the eitzah?

Is the setting correct for me to properly discuss this matter with him?

Do I have the proper amount of time for this type of discussion?

Is there a language barrier with the gadol with whom I wish to speak? And, if so, will it be possible for me to get proper guidance?

Will he understand that I want an eitzah — and not a berachah?

How well does the gadol know me? And, if he does not know me well, how can I give him a sense of who I am and the complete situation?

How much information does he need in order to understand my request for an eitzah properly?

Is he the right person to ask this question? Is this question within his area of expertise?

Will I be completely comfortable sharing all details of the request for an eitzah with this gadol?

Finally, am I completely open to listening to what he will tell me? To help yourself get in touch with your own feelings, ask yourself which of these three scenarios fit your inclination regarding the decision you are about to make.

My mind is already (or just about) made up.

I am leaning to one option more than to another, but am still unsure.

I am completely uncertain what to do.

It is important to understand that it is appropriate to approach a *gadol* with any of these three thoughts. But it is important for *you* and *the gadol* to know where you stand, as it will impact your framing of the question — and the *eitzah* that you receive from him.

Once you are ready to present your request for an *eitzah*, here are some practical tips:

PREPARE PROPERLY

*P*repare for your discussion properly. Compile a list of the questions that you want answered and frame your questions well. In my personal and professional life, whenever I have sought the *eitzah* of a *gadol*, I have found that preparing for the meeting was extremely helpful in clarifying my own thoughts.

A very important component of your preparation involves collecting all relevant information to help the *gadol* provide you with an *eitzah*. Consider the following incident that occurred with the Gerer Rebbe many years ago, as related by Rabbi Yehudah Rabinowitz, in his sefer, *Kerem Chemed* on *Meseches Berachos* (page 23).

A businessman came to the *Imrei Emes* for advice concerning a business deal. The *Imrei Emes* asked about the pros and cons of pursuing this venture, but the man did not have all the information.

The *Imrei Emes* replied that he had no advice for the man, either.

"It says in the *Gemara* that that leaders would take counsel from *Achitofel*, consult with the *Sanhedrin* and then ask the *Urim Vetumim*," he explained. "That means that first one should get expert advice, then ascertain whether the matter is *muttar* or *assur* and only afterward ask direction from *ruach hakodesh*" — meaning from the Rebbe.

BACKGROUND INFORMATION

*P*lease share background information that the *gadol* will need to know in order to understand your request for an *eitzah*. If you are a close *talmid* of your *Rosh Yeshivah*, or a *chassid* of a particular Rebbe, you may assume that the *gadol* knows you well. But if this is not the case, please see to it that you afford him a window into your life in order to enable him to properly address your request.

I would also strongly suggest that you begin with an introductory sentence or two that will clearly articulate what it is that you wish the *gadol* to address.

Some examples:

We would like an eitzah regarding the possibility of our family making aliyah.

We were given certain advice regarding our teenage son. We would like to share them with the Rosh Yeshivah and get his guidance.

I am about to leave Kollel and enter the business world. Can the Rav give me a berachah?

Let me give you the perspective of someone on the other side of the table (or *shtender*): When parents call me for advice regarding an at-risk teen, for example, I rarely find out what it is that they wish from me until they make their closing request. (Are they looking for a school-placement recommendation, a referral for a therapist, help in deciding if they should take the young man out of yeshivah and send him to work, or any of many other possibilities?) Having this introductory information provided at the beginning of our conversation would reduce my level of concern and allow me to concentrate better on the parts of the discussion that are most relevant to their request. I try to begin the conversation by gently inquiring what it is that the person(s) came to request of me, but some people get flustered, thinking that I am rushing them.

THE PROPER SETTING IS CRITICAL

I would venture to say that most of my friends who are in their 40's and 50's would not be able to maintain the punishing schedule of our *gedolim* for one week, let alone for years on end. Our *roshei yeshivah* and senior *rabbanim*, most of them well past retirement age, are overburdened with the demands of their mosdos and the needs of the *Klal*. (See Shiya Markowitz's excellent article on the need to protect and preserve our *gedolim*, "Torah Leadership: A National Resource or Public Property?" *JO*, Feb. '92.)

I do not have any suggestions to remedy this situation, but it is important that you understand that if you wish to seek the guidance of the top tier of our *gedolim*, you should consider finding the proper setting for a discussion that will allow you *yishuv hada'as* — reflective time.

Call the Rosh Yeshivah and ask for an appointment. Travel to his yeshivah if that works best for him. "Buttonholing" a *gadol* in a noisy wedding hall simply is not good practice. In all likelihood, if you do meet in a hectic setting, he may logically assume that you are seeking a *berachah*, and you may walk away thinking that you received an *eitzah*.

LANGUAGE

*C*onsider the language and comfort-level factor when preparing to present your request for an *eitzah*. Are you fluent in the language of the *gadol*, and are you completely comfortable discussing every aspect of this matter with him? Often asking for an *eitzah* requires you to share highly personal matters and feelings with an *adam gadol* — something that is quite difficult to do. Bear in mind that there are some *gedolim* with whom you may have a greater comfort level, and it may be wiser to seek their assistance.

My *chaver*, Rabbi Yosef Chaim Golding, shared a poignant story with me regarding a *gadol's* approach to providing an *eitzah* when the presenter had a language barrier.

> In the early years of JEP (Jewish Education Program) in the late 1970's, Rabbi Mutty Katz and he met with Rabbi Yaakov Kamenetsky z'tl to pose several she'ilos regarding working with Jewish public school and other assimilated children.
>
> Rabbi Golding, who was not perfectly fluent in Yiddish, asked Rav Yaakov if he could ask the questions in English.
>
> Rav Yaakov shook his head "no," and pointed to one of the rebbei'im present in the room. "Ask your she'ilos to him in English," said Rav Yaakov," and then he will translate them into Yiddish for me.
>
> Before answering, Rav Yaakov asked Rabbi Golding if the translator presented the questions correctly and only then did he respond.

It is important to note that the language barrier may not make much difference in the case of a *berachah*, but it is very relevant in the case of an *eitzah*. Permit me to be so bold as to say that it is nearly impossible to get a proper *eitzah* if there is a significant language barrier. In fact, one of the reasons that the members of the Sanhedrin needed to be fluent in all seventy languages was to insure that they would properly understand the words — and nuances — of the witnesses and litigants who appeared before them.

ALL PARTIES PRESENT

*O*ne final point on the setting and preparation for a request for an *eitzah*. It is good practice for all parties to be present, if possible, when the request is posed. If, for example, parents are requesting *hadrachah* for raising their child, I feel that both parents should be present when speaking to the *gadol* — even though the father may have a greater comfort level speaking to him.

There are several reasons for this. First, the *gadol* may have probing questions that will help him better understand the facts on the ground. And to be perfectly candid, mothers are usually more in tune with the needs and realities of their children. Additionally, on a very practical level, these types of *eitzos* require tough decisions to be made. Hearing the *eitzah* firsthand often provides a greater comfort level for the mother and makes her feel more empowered in the process of the request for the *eitzah*.

AREA OF EXPERTISE

*I*magine the following scenario that requires you to seek an *eitzah*:

You are a very successful real-estate developer. In order to inspire the confidence of your investors, banking officials, and potential sellers who want to be sure that you can close the deal, it is important that you wear expensive suits and drive a very luxurious automobile.

It would be entirely proper and appropriate for you to consult with your Rosh Yeshivah and ask him if it is congruous with your *hashkafos* (Torah-value system) to display such conspicuous consumption. But it would be foolish and pointless to ask a *gadol* if you ought to look into a Cadillac or a Lexus!

I purposely used an extreme example to illustrate my point that *gedolim* should not be asked questions that are outside their sphere of knowledge. But there are many more subtle instances where *gedolim* are asked to give *eitzos* in arenas that are far outside the area of their expertise.

Take *chinuch* matters, for example. Some *gedolim* and *roshei yeshivah* are very knowledgeable about learning disabilities and the courses of action designed to remediate them. Some are not acquainted with the available options. That does not diminish their status as *gedolei olam*. It just means that they are not experts in the area and therefore not the best ones to consult if you are seeking advice on dealing with a child who has a problem.

Another example would be in the arena of at-risk teens. There are many *eitzos* that could and should be asked of our *gedolim* and many *she'ilos* that should be asked of a *posek* when one is raising a teenager who is going through a difficult phase (see following paragraphs). However, this does not mean that this *gadol* or *rav* has a deep understanding of clinical depression, chemical addictions, or compulsive gambling.

THE PROPER SEQUENCE

*P*lease note that I am not suggesting that a *gadol* should not be consulted to guide parents and *mechanchim*. They most certainly should — **after all relevant information to frame the question has been gathered.**

In one of the examples noted above regarding the child with a learning disability, the proper course of action for parents would be to have the child tested for disabilities by a competent and professionally trained expert. The next step should be for the parents to explore all options as to choices for meeting the educational needs of this child. Armed with this information, the parents should then consult a *rav/gadol* for an *eitzah*.

A proper sequence of action would result in informed parents asking for thoughtful and appropriate *eitzos*:

We did our homework and the best educational setting for my child is to attend a yeshivah setting with children who are exposed to secular culture far more than our children, or for the child *le'havdil* to spend 45 minutes each day learning to read in a specialized program in the local public school. Which is more important — *"chevrah"* or a better educational setting?

Our son suffers from clinical depression. The doctors say that we should not be putting pressure on him while he is in therapy. Should we be waking him for *minyan* if he resists our efforts to do so? How about asking him to put on *tefillin*? How do we balance his needs with our value system at home and his influence on our younger children?

WHY DON'T THEY TELL US THAT?

*Y*ou may respond to these last few paragraphs with a reasonable question. If I ask a *gadol* for an *eitzah* in an area outside his expertise, why won't he simply tell me to seek advice elsewhere?

The answer is that they usually do tell you to go elsewhere for advice. I have noticed, however, that the majority of people either do not understand what they are being told and get frustrated at what they perceive to be a polite brush-off, or simply do not take "no" for an answer.

One of my close friends recently related to me that he once called *Mori V'Rabi* Horav Avrohom Pam *z'tl* to discuss the high school placement of his teenage daughter. Rav Pam listened for a while, offered him some general advice, and suggested that he contact someone who knows his daughter and who would be more knowledgeable about the local high school options for girls. My *chaver* told me that he felt disappointed at first, not getting the answer he was seeking. After reflection, however, he realized that he had asked my *Rebbi* a question that was beyond the area of his experience.

Additionally, some people are simply in too much pain to be able to understand. Take the case of desperate parents who go to a *rosh yeshivah* for help with a rebellious teenager and who are basically told that he cannot help them other than to empathetically listen and offer them a *berachah* — and perhaps a referral. *But you are the Gadol Hador,* they think. *How could you not be able to help us? If not you, then who can help us?*

The simple answer (or question) is: How *should* he be able to help you al *regel achas* (in the course of one session) — and without meeting with your child? The circumstances that led to this teenage defiance did not appear overnight and will, in all likelihood, take months or years to remediate, even in the hands of a trained professional.

Our caring, devoted *gedolim* deeply understand their role and carry the burden of the *Klal* magnanimously. They are sensitive human beings who are also parents and grandparents. They truly are *nosei ba'ol* (they empathize with you and share your pain) and feel equally frustrated when you ask them for an *eitzah* that they cannot assist you with.

It is of utmost importance, therefore that you clarify what it is that you wish from a *gadol* before you make the appointment — and see to it that you have a realistic set of objectives.

INDIVIDUAL NATURE — AND OWNERSHIP — OF AN *EITZAH*

*A*nother area where guidance is helpful in the arena of requesting *hadrachah* is developing an understanding of the individual nature — and ownership — of your requests. To begin with, you cannot *"pasken* from a *p'sak"* — meaning you cannot assume that the guidance given to one family can automatically be extrapolated to address the needs of any other family. Additionally, it is vitally important to understand that the guidance given to the *Klal* is by nature very different than that which is tailored for an *individual.* And it is the obligation of the individual — or those acting on behalf of that individual — to reflect upon, and if needed, pose the personalized request for an *eitzah.*

Take the issue of full-time learning for a *bachur* or *yungerman,* for example. Virtually all *rabbonim* and *gedolim* in the yeshivah world will advocate full-time learning for *bachurim,* and, to varying degrees, for *yungerleit* after their wedding. At the same time, the vast majority of our *gedolim* will suggest a part or full-time school or work environment for young men above a certain age who are clearly not cut out for full-time learning. In fact, many of our leading *gedolim* have made similar adjustments for their own children, grandchildren, and sons of their closest *talmidim.* My point is that it is the sacred obligation of *parents* to assess each of their children *as individuals* and help them chart a course for their lives that is appropriate for them. And it is the parents who should be requesting *eitzos* on behalf of their children. In a similar vein, it is the responsibility of each couple to closely and carefully assess their family unit and, when needed, ask for an *eitzah* or a *p'sak* from their *Rav* regarding matters that are highly personal in nature.

IN CLOSING

The *gedolei Yisrael* are wise and perceptive people who have spent years steeped in Torah study. Their guidance reflects not only their personal acumen and experience, but also their *Da'as Torah* — an expression of their vast Torah knowledge. Their opinion must therefore represent to us how we, as Jews, are expected to act.

On the other hand, their advice is based on the information presented to them, so when we turn to them for guidance, it is up to us to be certain that we have properly done our job.

Maintaining a *kesher* with one's *rebbi* is an obligation on the individual, as the Mishnah clearly states *Asei l'cha rav* (accept upon yourself a *rav*, *Avos* 1:6). With the exponential growth of the size of our largest yeshivos, it is more important than ever for each person and family to nurture and maintain a close bond with a *rav* or *rosh yeshivah*. Doing so will enable you to get the *eitzos* (and *berachos*) you will need as you travel on life's journey and seek to fulfill your dreams.

Chapter Two

AN OUNCE OF PREVENTION

REACHING TODAY'S UNDERACHIEVERS BEFORE THEY BECOME TOMORROW'S DROP-OUT TEENS

*W*e are faced with a critical problem, one that we must address as a society. There is a spiritual underclass that exists in our community: drop-out teens. This group of teenagers has no defining prerequisites; they come from every type of home, and every income level. These are children that *mechanchim* (educators), parents — indeed society as a whole — have failed to reach. In Monsey alone, there are dozens of such boys ages 16 and above who are in no yeshivah setting at all. We bump into them at the mall, and we catch sight of them through the plate-glass window of the pool hall. In the Greater New York area there are hundreds. And their numbers are growing. Rapidly.

On analysis, only a small percentage of these boys (and girls) have extenuating circumstances that may have contributed to their difficulties. Some come from very trying home situations. Others of a more intellectual bent have serious questions of faith that *r"l* led them astray. The vast majority, however, have but one thing in common. They have never felt successful in yeshivah. Shuffling from class to class, or worse yet, from school to school, their frustration grows to intolerable levels. Parental pressure increases; they often feel incredibly inadequate compared to their siblings; their self-confidence shrinks and often disappears. When they attempt to assert themselves at home or in school, it is often in awkward and inappropriate ways. This leads to more rebuke, more slings and arrows attacking their already low self-image.

This downward spiral continues until the child reaches eighth grade, and the harrowing search for a mesivta begins in earnest. After a rejection from the local mesivta, the parents frantically begin to research yeshivos geared to the underachieving student. For some the search ends there. For others, their parents fear that this type of yeshivah places a stigma on their son. Hopefully the child is accepted to his second or third choice of yeshivah high school. If this does not happen, this sensitive teenager is forced to admit to his peers that he has no idea which yeshivah will accept him. While his classmates are excitedly making summer plans, he is in limbo regarding his status for the coming school year. By the time his parents have placed him in yeshivah, his self-image has suffered yet another body blow.

If this trend does not reverse itself in ninth or tenth grade, new dynamics enter the equation. A driver's license. Work. A social life. Suddenly this young adult who has never been made to feel valuable or appreciated before, is told what a wonderful job he does, how charming he is etc .... At this point we have entered a new phase in the struggle for this *Yiddishe neshamah* (Jewish soul); a very difficult uphill battle.

A CALL TO ACTION

*T*wo *rebbei'im* in Monsey have heeded the call of the local *rabbanim*, and have formed a wonderful series of nightly *shiurim* (classes) geared to such young men and their specific needs. To call this program a success would be an understatement. The *shiurim* are generally well attended and sparked by much genuine enthusiasm. Most important is the opportunity that presents itself for these *bachurim* (youngsters) to bond with a *rebbi*. Frequently, these *shiurim* are followed by heart-to-heart conversations with the *rebbi* lasting well into the night.

A monumental difference exists between *our* "drop-out teens" and those of the secular world. While the external trappings of these boys are not those of the average *yeshivah bachur*, there is a genuine thirst for spirituality in these young men. What is outstanding is the devotion these *bachurim* have for their *rebbei'im* and for one another. Often the boys themselves approach one of the *rebbis*, offering to contribute to the rent money for the facilities that they use. Every wedding of a member of the group is celebrated with great *simchah* by all. They have developed a remarkable sense of unity that cuts across the greatly divergent backgrounds from which they come.

The secret to the success of this program is that the dedicated *rebbei'im*, all volunteers, follow a simple set of guidelines; one that can be instrumental in making our own contact with these youngsters successful. Don't be judgmental or condescending. Speak to them with respect. Don't comment on their appearance. Never, ever, attempt witty cracks or humorous lines at their expense. Just accept them for what they are; nice kids going through a difficult time.

A CHILDHOOD SQUANDERED

The most bittersweet feeling when observing this phenomenon is: Why couldn't we have reached these children five or eight years earlier, and avoided all this heartache? Each "client" represents so much strife within the family, so many sleepless nights for the parents, so much turmoil and pain within the boy's psyche, so much unrealized potential for growth; indeed, a childhood squandered. We must collectively examine this situation carefully and search for meaningful changes that we can implement to reverse this frightening trend.

Each situation, taken separately, lends itself to a logical explanation. When viewing the broad picture, however, it becomes glaringly obvious that something is very, very wrong. About one child you'll hear, "Of course he rebelled; look at how strict his parents are." Yet regarding another young man in the same situation, you hear, "Growing up in such a permissive environment can only lead to trouble."

"I begged his parents not to spoil him like that" versus "Are you surprised that he ran off to work? Look at how poor his family is!"

"Could you imagine the pressure he feels growing up with such an esteemed father?" versus "Like father like son — he never had a role model at home. What do you expect?"

It is true that for many families, there is a crisis in their children's *chinuch* (education) world. But the two *rebbei'im* in Monsey show that help is possible. Our challenge is to expand the program and bring it to every child who needs it.

SEARCHING FOR CAUSES

What then, has changed so dramatically? For one thing, the moral level of the secular world at large has been in an unrestrained free fall for many years now. In the 14 years that I have been teaching eighth graders, the decadence they are exposed to has increased not incrementally, but exponentially. And its shows. Even those who do not have a television set at home cannot shield their children from the relentless barrage of depravity that permeates every face of secular society. But, despite our best efforts, we cannot completely shield our children from this onslaught.

So what we must address is a problem that we can help remediate. Throughout the past generation, we have been, *Baruch Hashem*, raising the expectation level of what our yeshivah system should produce as a final product. Yeshivos are not merely satisfied with graduating a group of young men who will attend a *shiur* and support the local yeshivah. Our goal is to graduate lay leaders who can give the *shiurim*, and *yungeleit* (*kollel* fellows) who have the ability to become the *roshei hayeshivah*. We as *mechanchim* are rightfully thrilled by this development. Our yeshivah-educated parent body demands it, and we eagerly do everything in our power to accede to their requests.

THE CRESCENDO OF TAUNTS

The harsh reality is that a substantial number of our children cannot keep up with these demands. Try as they may, many of them are unable to meet these higher expectations. As we ratchet up the tension level and raise the bar to encourage them to hurdle to greater heights, many of these children crash into the bar time and time again. Broken hearted and discouraged, they simply stop trying and seek fulfillment elsewhere.

The haunting story of Elisha Ben Avuyah — *Acher* — comes to mind. Acher had sinned and the door to *teshuvah* was closed to him. He heard a *Bas Kol*, a heavenly voice, which proclaimed: *"Shuvu banim shovavim chutz me'Acher."* The voice informed him that all were welcome to repent except for him. His response was *"Hoyil ... lis'hani behai alma."* He replied, "Since the option of repentance is not available to me, I will at least derive pleasure from this world," and he *r'l* returned to his path of sin.

These sensitive young men are misreading our well-intentioned messages to them. They are not hearing our calls to improve, they misconstrue the pleas of their parents to better their lives and enrich their futures. All that keeps reverberating in their ears is the never-ending imaginary shout of voices that pierce their hearts: "You can't make it in our classroom, in our yeshivah, in our mesivta, in our home ..."

SEARCHING FOR SOLUTIONS

*I*t is not my intent to offer broad solutions to this complex problem. For that we defer, as always, to our *gedolim*. I would humbly like to share with other *mechanchim* some of the methods that — combined with the *tefillah* and *seyata diShmaya* — I have found to be helpful in these situations.

1) Convey to your *talmidim* (students) again and again that each of them has a contribution to make to *Klal Yisrael*. We all had classmates who struggled in yeshivah and became outstanding adults. Share some anecdotes with some of the weaker *talmidim* in a private setting. This past year, when I had quite a few *talmidim* who were not learning

well and were very frustrated, I was speaking to the entire class about overcoming adversity. A *talmid* respectfully asked me, "What do you know about difficulty?"

I immediately responded, "You obviously never met my eighth-grade *rebbi*."

When the laughter subsided, and I saw that he was not satisfied, I softly informed the class that I had had a speech impediment — stuttering — as a child and I had to go to therapy to correct this problem. They were shocked. They also didn't believe me. I told them to think back carefully and remember that often when teaching a difficult piece of *Gemara*, I often let my guard down and stutter a bit. It made such an impression on them that several parents called that night thanking me for sharing my infirmity with the children, and how validating it was for their son to know that their *rebbi* had to overcome shortcomings of his own.

2) The Parent-Teacher Conference affords an important opportunity to review the accomplishments of the *talmid* with his parents, and discuss areas that need improvement. It has its limitations, however. The conference is generally conducted in December, after much of the semester has passed. There is precious little "quality time" for a serious, protracted discussion of the situation. Most of all, the most important element of this dialogue is missing: the student.

Three years ago, I experimented with a new technique for helping *talmidim* who were not learning according to their ability. The week after Sukkos, I invited the parents of one such *talmid* to my home and requested that their son come along. We scheduled the meeting for late evening, when their younger children (and mine) were sleeping. We spent approximately a full hour discussing many issues pertaining to the child's education and social interaction. The improvement in the boy's learning was remarkable.

Since then, I have been doing this with all *talmidim* that are not performing at their level. I have yet to conduct such a meeting and fail to see a dramatic improvement in the boy's attitude and learning.

3) We teachers must stop the destructive habit of obtaining a scouting report on our *talmidim* before the school year begins. One would have to be superhuman not to let negative information taint the way we treat the incoming class. Children start a new school with hope and expectations that problems of the past will remain in the past. Speak to many of the teenage "problem kids." You will hear this refrain again and again: "I was never given a fair chance after my first bad year." There just may be some truth to it. How many times have we heard the warning, "Watch out for — [a particular child]?"

In the spirit of fairness, let us imagine that we were told negative information about the **best** student in the class. Picture the scenario. The star *talmid* raises his hand the very first day to ask a splendid question on the day's *Gemara* lesson. The *rebbi* hears warning bells. ("They were right about this kid; he's starting up already!")

It is critical for a *rebbi* to have certain information about his *talmidim* before the year begins, but only to ascertain which students require more sensitive handling. If a child has a sick parent or sibling or if the child comes from a challenging home situation, etc, these facts must be conveyed to a *rebbi*.

When a new group of *talmidim* enters the classroom, the first thing that the *rebbi* should tell them is that he knows nothing about them, and that he has no interest in their past performance.

4) Parents, teachers, and other authority figures at times hold up children for embarrassment or shame in front of classmates, siblings, or friends. Callously shaming a child in front of his friends can leave emotional scars and anger that smolder for years. On the other hand, words of admonishment that are offered with love and understanding, respecting the child's feelings and need for privacy, will be received accordingly.

5) A dress code is an integral part of the structure of any yeshivah. Indeed, it is often a defining element in the school; as such, the yeshivah has the obligation to enforce these rules vigorously. When the child runs afoul of these guidelines, however, it can be a source of great conflict between a *talmid* and his *rebbi*, so it is time for the *rebbi* to exit gracefully. A *rebbi* cannot afford to squander all of his political capital and enter an adversarial relationship with a *talmid* over the length of the child's hair, size of his yarmulke, etc.

   I strongly suggest that if it becomes obvious that these violations are not isolated incidents, but rather indicate a rebellious pattern, it would be appropriate for the administration of the yeshivah to step in. To be sure, parents must assume responsibility and support the yeshivah's position. Without this crucial backing, the yeshivah will find it quite impossible to resolve this situation painlessly.

6) Within a heterogeneous group, much can be done to accommodate the educational and social needs of the *talmid* who is encountering difficulty.

   Tests can be a source of great stress for the underachiever. On a temporary basis, it is often helpful to allow the child to be tested on a small portion of the material covered (1 *blatt* out of 4; until *Sheini* in *Chumash*). Insist that he does well on that amount. After you have built up his self-confidence, he will be able to be accountable for larger amounts.

If a student is obviously unable to read the *Gemara* or *Chumash*, perhaps assure him that in the short term you will not call on him to read publicly. Or better yet, give him a short piece to prepare, and only then call on him to say this piece. He will be grateful to you for caring about his feelings and his desire to learn will increase tenfold.

Another helpful idea is to allow the child to take notes during class and then use them during the written exam. Insist that they must be *his* notes only; don't allow him to copy from the other boys. You will be training him to be focused and involved in the daily class.

Much tact is needed to avoid incurring the envy of the other students. One way to deal with this is by reserving the top echelon of report-card grades for those who do not resort to any of these aids. Generally speaking, the other students will respect the fact that you are dealing gently with their peers. You also will be teaching them a valuable lesson in *derech eretz,* understanding, and tolerance.

TO TRACK OR NOT TO TRACK

There has always been a heated debate among *mechanchim* whether the larger *yeshivos*, those that have two classes or more in each grade level, should "track" the *talmidim* (grouping them according to ability) or not. Those who disagree with the tracking method cite two valid reasons:

a) The presence of *talmidim* who excel in their *limudim* (studies) gives average performers a goal to aim for. Indeed, lack of boys that are *"shteiging"* (advancing) could lead to lowered expectations, resulting in weaker children not performing in accordance with their even limited abilities. Additionally, the presence of a stronger group of *talmidim* is often a positive influence in terms of *yiras Shamayim*: they *daven* better etc.

To deprive weaker *talmidim* of this positive peer pressure is unfair and undermines their future. Why should we compromise the goals of these *talmidim* just because they find learning difficult? The often-quoted decision in this matter is from Rabbi Aharon Kotler *z'tl,* who advised school heads not to remove weaker students from the class, and maintained that they will, with the passage of time, integrate with the other *talmidim* and remain devoted to Torah and *mitzvos*.

b) We do not live in a Utopian society. The brutal reality is that these children become labeled as soon as they are placed in a slower track. They feel inadequate, no mesivta will take them, and they will become second-class citizens. Principals fear a bruising battle with each parent who is informed of the decision to track his/her son.

c) It happens very often that the relative levels of achievement change with time. Children may not have a very good memory or natural reading skills to excel in lower grades, but undetected learning skills may develop as the child gets older, and vice versa.

RETHINKING THE ISSUES

*P*erhaps the time has come to rethink our opposition to this system. Let us address the first two factors mentioned. First the educational concerns:

We will begin with the decision of Rav Aharon. As explained to me by Rabbi Yehoshua Silbermintz *z'l,* who discussed this issue personally with Rav Aharon, the *Rosh Yeshivah* was addressing a totally different situation. The question posed was: "At what point does the yeshivah/*rebbi* have the authority to ask a disruptive child to leave the yeshivah/classroom?" To which Reb Aharon replied that if the presence of a *talmid* is so detrimental to the general atmosphere by his conduct or by eroding the moral compass of others, the yeshivah has the right, indeed the obligation, to remove him before he harms others.

The next question posed was what to do with a boy who casts a pall over the classroom — not by disruption, but by lack of effort or inability to keep up.

It was in this context that the poignant *p'sak,* "Let a weak *talmid* remain and listen," was issued. So this decision has little bearing on our discussion.

I do not advocate departmentalizing *Limudei Kodesh* (religious subjects). Torah is handed down from *rebbi* to *talmid.* It is difficult enough to maintain a close relationship with 25 students, let alone 75. We can, however, structure all or some of our classes — especially *Gemara shiurim* — to create homogenous groups so that the underachieving student can be educated appropriately. This would also alleviate the very real problem of bright students who are developing poor study habits in mainstream classes where they are frustrated by being forced to endure long stretches of review sessions on the new *Gemara* lessons that they so quickly and eagerly devour. Which brings us to the social issue:

Without question, it is hurtful for a child to be informed that he belongs in a weaker class. However, this temporary discomfort will pass. Children adapt to all situations. This cannot begin to compare to the ongoing pain of knowing you are not growing, the agony of that walk to the *rebbi's* desk to pick up your test paper, the dread of being called upon to read the *Gemara* in public.

The major difficulty is getting parents on board. I firmly believe that parents will be willing partners in this endeavor if we can convince them that these changes are designed for the benefit of their sons, rather than to alleviate the yeshivah's own problems. If they are still unhappy, we must have the courage of our convictions. Our job is to decide what is in the child's best interest and then to act. We cannot be in the position of reacting to the polling data regarding the popularity of a decision on such an important issue. At the end of the day, parents want what the school wants: a happy, motivated, well-adjusted child. When parents witness their child's progress, they will agree that we made the correct decision.

A REWARDING CHALLENGE FOR THE RIGHT REBBI

A word to *rebbei'im* who might have the inclination to teach a tracked class geared to the underachieving *talmid*: by all means do so!

If your *menahel* is opposed to the idea, plead with him to try it just once. Prepare yourself for this task by getting as much educational training as possible. However, what you really need is to love your *talmidim*, and believe — truly believe — that there are no bad children. Your *talmidim* will pick up on this feeling and give you the utmost. It will be the most rewarding experience of your *chinuch* life.

Yes, you will miss that delightful feeling of starting a *Beis Halevi* [an advanced Torah thought] and watching the brilliant *talmid* jump up and finish it for you, all the while giving you that 100-watt smile. Your successes will seem very small at the onset, but they will without question grow as the year progresses. Most of all, that wonderful feeling of knowing you turned a young man's life around forever will be yours for the rest of your life.

You must be made aware of the drawbacks of teaching a class such as this. You will be genuinely sad when the year ends — you'd love to have just a bit more time to work on the diamond that you discovered and polished so very carefully. You will worry about your *talmidim* — long after they have left your class — in a way you never thought you could. You will find yourself calling their present *rebbei'im* to plead with them to have a soft touch with your *talmid*. Every *bein hazmanim* (yeshivah intersession), as soon as the boys return home from yeshivah, they will drop in to say hello. Former *talmidim* will call you every Friday afternoon to wish you, "A *gutten Shabbos*." Every Purim, until they go off to *Eretz Yisrael*, or get married, they will be at your home with *mishloach manos*.

You see, you aren't becoming **a** *rebbi* of theirs; hopefully you will become **the** *rebbi* — the one who they will remember for the rest of their lives.

Chapter Three

A POUND OF CURE

The telephone rang. A woman was calling to discuss her concerns regarding her 17-year-old son. After a minute or two, she began sobbing uncontrollably as she described his downward slide throughout his high school years. The "bad friends," the constant bickering with his parents over dozens of issues large or small, the tension and friction with his siblings, being asked to leave the four yeshivos that he had attended during those three years. Now he had hit rock bottom.

During the past six weeks, he refused to even consider enrolling in yet another yeshivah. He sleeps until noon, "hangs around the house" until suppertime, then, with a curt farewell, leaves home. He returns in the early hours of the morning, goes to sleep, and begins the next day in the same fashion as the previous ones. Any attempt by his parents to determine where or with whom he is spending his time is met with a disrespectful or downright rude retort. Her voice became practically inaudible as she described the events of that particular morning. She had entered his room in a futile attempt to wake him up for Shacharis. He became verbally abusive to her, and ordered her out of his room, even threatened her. "Rabbi Horowitz," she cried, "my son was the sweetest child you could imagine. Now I am afraid that he is becoming clinically depressed. What should I do?!?"

At this point, it was obvious to me that due to the mother's distress, a serious, protracted discussion was impossible. After a few more minutes of conversation, I hung up the telephone, with the promise of returning the call as soon as possible.

REFLECTION

*L*ater that evening, I began the second conversation by asking the woman how many times she had asked her son any of the following questions that day:

"Why aren't you going to yeshivah?"

"Why are you wasting your time?"

"When are you finally going to do something with your life?"

She mumbled an evasive response. I politely informed her that it would be simply impossible for me to assist her without her complete cooperation. She hesitantly answered "About ten or fifteen times."

Fifteen times six (days) equals ninety comments per week. Ninety times six weeks totals five hundred and forty hurtful attacks on her son's self-confidence. I explained to the woman that although her son's disrespectful behavior is inexcusable, she must keep in mind that he is in as much agony as she is, perhaps more so. He feels that no yeshivah actually wants him, and that he has nowhere to go. Each time that she reminded him of this painful fact, she was inadvertently causing him needless anguish, and adding to the chasm that exists between them. His antisocial behavior is his clumsy response to his perception (real or imagined) that our society has rejected him.

After extracting a promise from her to refrain from any further barbs directed to her son, I offered to meet him in my home on Sunday afternoon. I told her to simply inform her son that I am a placement counselor who assists teenagers.

HARD QUESTIONS

A handsome, well-dressed young man swaggered into my study. After making small talk for a few minutes, I began by discussing his secular education. He has only completed the second year of high school (he maintained an 85 average), and is currently not enrolled in any program at all. I asked him if he has any computer skills; he answered that he does not. I chided him for not pursuing his quest for a high school diploma, or at least a G.E.D. (an equivalency diploma). He was very agreeable, and we spend several minutes discussing his options.

We then shifted the conversation to his *limudei kodesh* pursuits. He grew visibly agitated as we discussed the reasons for his failure to achieve success in yeshivah. He conceded that he was often uncooperative and had "an attitude" during his past two school placements, despite having caring rabbis who truly tried to communicate with him. I then probed into the current situation.

"Why don't you make a serious effort to find a yeshivah where you can grow intellectually?" I asked.

"No yeshivah wants me; and even if I got accepted, I'm just not cut out for learning."

I informed him that I disagree with both statements. Besides, I asked him, "What do your parents say to this?"

"My mother said that I should join a yeshivah; any yeshivah, so that I can do a decent *shidduch*."

"What do you say to this? I asked.

"I refuse to waste my life. If I am not going to be successful in school, I'm better off just not going at all."

We sit quietly for a few moments. I then tell him, "You never told this to your parents in the manner that you are speaking to me now."

"How do you know?", he angrily asked me.

"I softly responded, "That's obvious. They keep asking you to go to yeshivah. You have convinced me in a few minutes that with your current mind-set, you will be unable to achieve success in any yeshivah. You haven't done that with them yet."

He then admitted that throughout the past few difficult and stressful months, he has not had one serious conversation with his parents. All dialogue takes place in midst of a shouting match about any one of a host of flash points in their relationship.

ROUND TWO

I changed the subject. "Nice shirt you're wearing."

"Thanks."

"How much did it cost you?"

"Twenty-four bucks. It's a forty-dollar shirt, but I got it at a closeout."

"How many hours did you have to work to pay for that shirt?" I innocently ask.

"Wadda you mean? My parents give me ..."

Ignoring the now hostile stare, I inform him that common decency requires that as long as he is spending his parents' money and eating at their table, he should inform them of his whereabouts when he leaves home at night even if they will be annoyed at his choice of destination. A telephone call home before his parents' bedtime informing them that he is safe, and when he will be returning home will help calm their nerves. Additionally, he should be more considerate of his parents' feelings when engaging in antisocial behavior in or near their home. This last comment drew a swift and passionate response.

"I couldn't care less what anyone thinks of me!" he forcefully said.

"In that case, why don't we exchange clothing with each other?" I ask with a smile (I wear traditional chassidic garb). "If you truly don't care what people think, it shouldn't be a problem." I hammer home the point. "You care greatly what your friends think of you. What you have made peace with is insulting your parents in front of their friends."

It was clearly time for a break, so I went out, made myself a cup of coffee, and we went for a walk. I asked him what yeshivah he plans to send his own sons to. He responded with the name of a Brooklyn yeshivah, similar to the one that he attended as a child (I'm not surprised; that is what most "drop-out teens" tell me. However, to the public at large, this response would be met with widespread disbelief.) "Are you aware that your parents are convinced that you are on the path to abandoning an Orthodox lifestyle?" I gently asked him.

"No way — they don't think that ... do they?" was his immediate and passionate response.

I responded, "You see, when I — and your parents — went to yeshivah, dropping out of school was almost immediately followed by an abandonment of Torah and mitzvos."

I told him that he would be well served to inform his parents of his ironclad commitment to an observant life, as it would reduce their anxiety greatly, and immeasurably lower the tension level at home. I then advised him to go home, take the telephone off the hook, and have a long talk with his parents about the many issues we discussed.

SOME POINTERS

After the young man left my house, I called his parents and gave them a quick primer on dealing with their son's crisis of confidence:

- אֵין חָבוּשׁ מַתִּיר עַצְמוֹ מִבֵּית הָאֲסוּרִים — A prisoner cannot extract himself from his bondage without the assistance of others (*Berachos* 5b). Do not hesitate to take advantage of the greatest asset that your community has — its dedicated *mechanchim* (or lay people) — and find someone whom your son can confide in and speak frankly with. Few teenagers, even in the best of situations, can do this with their parents.

- Establish an ongoing dialogue with him. That includes, but should not be limited to, serious discussions about present yeshivah and/or work possibilities, aspirations for the future, etc.

- Never discuss serious issues during an argument.

- Never, ever, engage in vicious, personal attacks on your son's friends when their names come up during an argument. First, despite your instructions to the contrary, every word that you utter will unquestionably be repeated to that friend. You will have earned yourself a sworn enemy at a time when you need every ally you can get. Additionally, bear in mind that, at this stage in your son's life, he is more closely aligned with his friends than he is with you. By attacking his friends, you are positioning them, and him, on the opposing side of a very formidable fence.

- Do not castigate yourselves as parents ("Where did we go wrong?"). This will accomplish nothing productive. The brutal reality is that these situations arise in every type of home and at every income level. More important, doing this in front of your son will only add to his feeling of inadequacy.

- After some time has passed, and you have established a working relationship, set a firm, but reasonable set of house rules for him, regarding his leaving and returning home at night. You will be pleasantly surprised by his response.

- Explain to him that you are willing to make some accommodations to meet the needs of his current lifestyle. However, ask him to understand that you have other children, parents, etc., and that he should be considerate of that reality as well. If you are unhappy with the music that he listens to, for example, ask him to close the door to his room, and insist that he wear headphones while the music is playing.

- Finally, think positively. The vast majority of these teens outgrow this temporary stage in their lives. One is reminded of the classic story of the 16-year-old who, after months of tension and fighting with his parents, ran away from home for a period of three years. Upon returning home, he remarked to his close friend that he just could not get over how much his parents matured during the time that he was away! Your son may not become everything that you had originally hoped for, but he will, with the help of Hashem, grow to be a wonderful adult; a source of *nachas* to himself, to you, and to *Klal Yisrael*.

HOPEFUL SIGNS

*S*everal weeks later, the young man described above calls me at home to thank me for assisting him. He is currently working part time, attending *shiurim* at a local yeshivah, and with the help of an accommodating *menahel,* working to achieve his high school diploma. He and his parents have spent many hours speaking to each other, and have met several times with their Rav to discuss the many issues at hand. By the way, he adds, things are much less stressful at home now. I smile, and thank the One Above for guiding me in formulating the proper responses for helping this young man.

I sit down to eat supper.

And the telephone rings again ...

Chapter Four

INDEPENDENT
COUNSEL

*I*t is an axiom in the mental health profession that the first step on the road to recovery is to avoid denial and squarely face the issue at hand.

In the past few years, our community has begun the painful process of evaluating the growing "at-risk teenager" crisis. The overwhelming majority of our boys and girls are achieving remarkable success in our excellent yeshivah and day school system, despite maintaining a rigorous dual curriculum of Hebrew and secular studies. There is, however, a small percentage of children who simply are unable to keep pace with the ever-increasing academic tempo of our schools. Frustrated and unhappy, they are very vulnerable to the entire gamut of antisocial behavior that affords them temporary gratification, the camaraderie of those who comprise the spiritual underclass that exists in communities across the country and who have opted out of the "system."

It is, without a doubt, naive to assume that there are simple solutions to such a complex issue. There is, however, one area where it is possible to effect significant improvement in the lives and future of many of these youngsters: by affording them the advice they so desperately need.

Having met with and counseled many hundreds of "at-risk teenagers" and their parents over the past decade, I am often struck by the fact that, in many or most of these situations, the kids are receiving little or no meaningful guidance from any adults at this most critical stage in their lives. True, well-meaning, loving parents and educators try to reach them, but in almost all instances, that (sound) advice is unsolicited and therefore is not treated with the respect that it deserves. The result? Teens are getting guidance from their peers and not from those best equipped to help them navigate the minefield of adolescence. This is a big problem.

One recent January, I was invited to deliver a short speech at the Yeshivah of Los Angeles Girl's High School. After I finished my remarks, I turned off the microphone, and casually mentioned to the girls that, in my opinion, most teens don't get enough guidance with issues that are troubling them. I also mentioned that one of the essential components of Project Y.E.S. is a hotline that I had recently initiated in the New York area to afford teens and their parents the venue to confidentially seek advice and guidance. I told the girls that if they have anything that they would like to ask me, they are welcome to do so.

After a few moments of silence, a young lady asked me what she should do to assist a friend of hers who, in her opinion, might be suffering from mild depression. I began by informing her that I have no professional training in this area. I then gave her some general guidelines for recognizing symptoms of depression, and suggested that she consult with the school principal, who would be glad to assist her with this matter.

For the next 30 minutes, with the entire student body and faculty present, I fielded questions on a wide range of topics, including school and general friendship issues, eating disorders, and effective methods for dealing with parents who are less religious (or more religious) than their children. The school principal then came to the podium and informed the girls that as long as they wished to remain in the auditorium and continue this impromptu give-and-take with me, classes would be canceled. The girls remained for an additional hour. After we concluded the session, several seniors approached me and asked me to meet with only the entire graduating class in order to discuss dating issues – with a *chassidic*-garbed Rabbi.

During my time with the senior class, I asked them why they do not actively seek guidance from the devoted and caring school faculty. (Indeed, it was evident to me – an outsider – that the administration and the faculty had an excellent relationship with the kids.) They conceded that almost all of them do some of the time, but it's hard to discuss personal matters with teachers who see you every day.

It is doubtlessly true that many teenagers speak in monosyllabic grunts that are only intelligible to other teens. (One parent told me that teen talk is similar to fax machines – the sounds that emanate from one of them are only intelligible to another one — but not to any other beings.) Nevertheless, most kids are desperately looking for someone to help them navigate this temporary but turbulent phase in their lives. The trick is to get your kids to seek your input. Easier said than done.

SOME PRACTICAL TIPS:

American jurisprudence affords the attorney-client privilege even to persons accused of committing the most heinous of crimes. The justification is a simple one. Lacking the comfort of discussing one's misdeeds freely with wiser people would preclude the alleged criminals from receiving the guidance that they so desperately need.

Often, when a child discusses his or her misdeeds with us, our knee-jerk reaction is to respond with a gasp or, worse yet, to severely admonish the child without allowing for a much-needed discussion of the issue(s) at hand. That does not mean that you should not express your opinion. Quite to the contrary, by offering a nonjudgmental ear, you will position yourself to offer thoughtful advice that your child will treasure.

Keep in mind that quite often this initial admission may be a "trial balloon" to try to gauge your reaction regarding a substantive topic that your child would love to be able to discuss with you. If you overreact to this initial incident, you can be assured that the next time around, it will be less likely that you or your spouse will be consulted regarding this matter.

Speak in words or sentences, not in chapters or books. We do not often capture the undivided attention of our kids. If you use this rare opportunity to recount every "sin"— real or imagined — committed during the past few years, you may find these opportunities becoming fewer and farther between. Focus on one message and keep it as short as possible.

Set limits. Never abdicate your responsibility. It is a grueling task to be in the position of having to say "no" to something that your child wishes to do. It is also your duty and obligation as a parent to do so.

Even if your son and daughter seem to resent the rules and moral choices that you impose on them, deep down, they greatly appreciate the guidance and direction that you are offering them. The kids intuitively know that all too often giving a young man or woman carte blanche means that his or her parents are not willing to spend the time and effort to teach their children right from wrong.

Perhaps the most important thing that you can do is to tender your children your unconditional love regardless of your level of disappointment with the choices they are making and the lives they are leading. This does not translate into tacit approval of their actions. In fact, this will afford you a greater voice in their lives.

In all my conversations with teenagers, the five words — uttered by youngsters with great bitterness and pain — that always render me speechless are, "My parents don't know me." Sadly, the kids are often correct. Please, please spend time with your children when they are young and eager to do so. You can be sure that once they enter their teenage years, the amount of time they will want to spend with you and the level of counsel they will seek from you will diminish to a mere fraction of what it once was. Train them at the youngest possible age to discuss their day and share their thoughts with you. As your children grow older, their inclination to discuss things freely with you will depend on their impression of how well you know them. Get to know them — really know them — and appreciate the unique qualities that each one of them possesses. You can be assured that if you will not learn to accept them for who they are — warts and all — others will be there to take your place. And you may not have the luxury of selecting who those replacements are.

Enjoy the formative years of your children's lives. Treasure every moment. Utilize your time with them to guide them, to mold them, to help them grow to be a source of *nachas* to themselves, to their families, and to all of *Klal Yisrael*.

Chapter Five

REPORT FROM GROUND ZERO

$\mathcal{I}$f we are going to have an impact on the frightening choice of some young men and women to abandon the teachings of our yeshivah and Bais Yaakov system, we will need to improve the overall quality of our home life. There is a common inclination to lay the blame for these problems on families in crisis. This type of thinking, however, does not do justice to such a difficult and complex issue. We must avoid the tendency to attribute all of the blame to "broken homes," and work to minimize the tension levels in *all* of our homes.

At the 1996 Agudath Israel National Convention, *Mori V'rabi* Rabbi Avrohom Pam, *z'tl* quoted the Steipler *z'tl* as having said, "*Hatzlachah mit kinder* (success with one's children) is 50 percent *shalom bayis* and 50 percent *tefillah*."

One thing is painfully clear. Our home life is under assault. It is not merely the unraveling of the moral fabric of secular society and its effect on (even) our insular community. *Our* homes are under assault. Longer work hours for both spouses, the exponential increase of our *simchah* schedules and social obligations, and the increased burden of providing *parnassah* for our growing families are taking their toll on the tranquility and *simchas hachayim (joie de vivre)* of our home life. Many of us are able to maintain this juggling act and keep all of these balls in the air at once. Many, however, are finding it very, very difficult.

Those who deal with at-risk teens almost unanimously agree that the greatest factor that puts children at risk is lack of *simchah* and *shalom bayis* (harmony) at home. Yes, some children just seem to be born "difficult." Some have an "ornery" disposition. Others have an innate propensity to challenge authority. Some are extremely restless and are simply not cut out for a 10-hour school day. Many have significant learning disabilities. Experience has shown, however, that children from warm, loving homes have the best chance of overpowering these difficulties and becoming well-adjusted adults despite having risk factors.

But children can never get used to bickering, stress, unhappiness, negative comments, and emotional abuse. These result in unhappy, distracted children who are unable to concentrate in school. They develop an intense distrust of authority figures, and harbor a simmering rage at an adult world that cannot seem to get its act together and provide them with a peaceful environment in which to grow up and thrive. This holds true for all households, including two-parent ones.

So, a short response to the frightened parents who ask for a short answer to what they can do to "protect" their family from the ravages of the counterculture that threatens their boys and girls can be found in the poignant comment of Rabbi Chaim Pinchas Scheinberg *shlita, Rosh Yeshivah* of Torah Ohr, that the most important thing that parents need to maintain in their home is a sense of happiness — *simchas hachayim*.

Ultimately, as vigilant as we must be to shield our children from the influences of secular society, our greatest defense against this onslaught is to create a happy and stable home life for our children. We must keep our eye on that goal and do everything possible in our power to see to it that the quality of our home life is as good as possible. It is not the intent of these lines to discuss the broad-based issues related to the topic of at-risk teens. We do, however, need to implement some initiatives and solutions that relate to the topic of this article: the improvement of our home life.

I. TRAINING

*D*uring *shanah rishonah* (the first year of married life) when a young couple is at the critical stage of developing their relationship, it should become the accepted societal norm for *both* spouses to attend a series of four, six, or perhaps eight classes on *shalom bayis*. Although the newlywed couple may not think so, this is the ideal time to do this. Young couples have a reasonable amount of discretionary time, and can begin to prepare their home to be a resting place for the *Shechinah* and a nurturing environment for their children to thrive in.

Many young men and women lack proper role models for establishing a relationship based on mutual respect and trust, or simply were not exposed to the positive influence of their parents' home during crucial years. Training helps. Education helps. More important, a good mentor will provide an opportunity for young couples to seek guidance when the inevitable bumps occur. Many couples are uncomfortable going to their parents and in-laws for direction at this critical stage in their lives.

As far as parenting is concerned, education is the key. It would be naïve to think that any one person has all the answers to the difficult questions that parenting presents. Many, many parents, however, have told me that their home life was immeasurably improved as a result of attending parenting workshops.

At a recent symposium, Rabbi Shmuel Kamenetsky, shlita, related the story of a young girl who was experiencing significant difficulty at home and in school. Professional counseling was recommended. After several sessions, a remarkable improvement was noted by all. Reb Shmuel related that the therapist told him that he had instructed the mother to take her daughter out of school for lunch in a restaurant and to spend at least one hour conversing with the girl, prior to each session. This, the therapist felt, was far more effective than his time with the young girl.

Similarly, it is great training for a young couple to spend time growing together as parents and sharing in the raising of their children. The practical tips and skills that are imparted at parenting classes greatly improve the quality of the home life as parents are trained to deal with the many issues and challenges that they face on a daily basis.

Yes, our parents seem to have done a decent job raising us without attending lectures or reading books, but times have changed and our children are faced with temptations that we never had. Good parenting skills do not always result in wonderful children. Effective parenting, however, can significantly improve the likelihood that a difficult child will grow up to become a well-adjusted, productive adult.

2. COMMUNITY

 woman approached a colleague of mine at a public gathering. She had been recently divorced and she asked

him to arrange for someone to take her school-age sons to *shul* on Shabbos. He related to me that his initial reaction was that a situation like this — where no one had come forward or arranged on their own to assist in this way — would be unthinkable in a small town or in a *kehillah*-type *shul* setting. People often speak about children falling through the cracks. The reality is that all too often, it is the families that are falling through the cracks.

In large metropolitan areas, where most Orthodox Jews live, one can *daven* in several *shuls* throughout the week without being a member in any of them. Although this may be very convenient for the individual *mispallel*, the family — lost in the anonymity of city life — forgoes the unique protection that the *kehillah* has to offer. An involved Rabbi and *Rebbetzin* guide young couples and their children through the inevitable difficulties that they will encounter. They are there to notice troubling tendencies in *shalom bayis*, in the *chinuch* of the children, or any one of a host of issues.

It is critical to the development of a Torah home that the family belong to a *kehillah*, attend *shiurim*, and above all, actively nurture a relationship with the Rabbi and *Rebbetzin* of the *shul*. Doing so will add many strands to the communal safety net that we all very much need.

3. SCHEDULES

*P*eople are always asking what has changed so dramatically (regarding the at-risk teen issue) in the past decade. There are some obvious answers — as well as more subtle ones. One of those that fall into the latter category is that we are more "stressed out" than any generation ever was. Please allow me to rephrase this. *We are not home enough.* Our family life is unraveling. We are working longer hours in more stressful situations. Perhaps much of this is unavoidable, due to the enormous pressure to provide *par-*

nassah for our growing families. One area, however, where significant improvement is not only possible but absolutely necessary is in our *simchah* schedules.

Our *gedolim* have — for years now — been requesting that we limit conspicuous consumption at our *simchos*. Although there are some exceptions, we have been reluctant, as a group, to take their advice. If we cannot or will not bite the bullet for the sake of a lifestyle of *tzeniyus*, then *asei lemaan tinnokos shel beis rabban* — let us do so for the sake of our children.

Every evening that we dress up after a busy workday and travel half an hour to wish a young couple *mazel tov* at a *lechayim* (to be followed by a *vort*, wedding, and *sheva berachos*), we are depriving our own children of desperately, desperately needed quiet time with us. While I am not recommending that we all become social dropouts and refuse to attend any *simchos*, it is clear that we need to limit our time away from home. Our primary obligation, after all, is to raise and nurture the children that *Hashem* blessed us with and with whose upbringing He has charged us.

4. *SHABBOS* AND *YOM TOV*

Shabbos Kodesh — A time for spiritual and emotional rejuvenation. A time for children, relaxation, and family. No telephone calls, no appointments, no distractions. Your children can now receive your individual attention as you, and they, unwind from the pressure-filled week. *Mei'ein Olam HaBa* (a taste of the World to Come).

Sadly, the hectic nature of our lives is unfortunately spilling over into the last bastion of our home life: *Shabbosos* and *Yamim Tovim*. After a 40-to-50-hour school week, when most children would treasure some downtime with their parents and family, or simply the luxury of being left alone to unwind, many are subjected to long

Shabbos meals with company present, where they are expected to behave in a picture-perfect manner. This, despite the fact that the entire conversation at the table is geared to the adults. Children who are naturally shy are pressured into reciting *divrei Torah* (*Torah thoughts*) in front of strangers. Parents go *Kiddush* hopping until well past noontime — with the unrealistic expectation of coming home to a clean home and relaxed children. Even more problematic, they leave their children with friends or relatives to attend weekend *Bar Mitzvahs*.

It is of great importance that we pause and take stock of our objective for our *Shabbosos*. We must strive to create this zone of *menuchah* (tranquility) in our homes at least once a week, so that our children can relax and look forward to this special day with their family.

DEALING WITH DIVINE

Allow me to state the obvious. Children are best served by growing up in a two-parent household. *Chazal's* comment that the *mizbei'ach* "sheds tears" when a couple divorces needs no elaboration. Having said that, divorce in and of itself does not consign a child to a bleak educational and social future. While statistically children from broken homes are in a high-risk category, it is only so, in my opinion, when there is strife and unhappiness in the child's life. Children can adjust to the painful reality of growing up in a single-parent household, when *both* parents maturely put their own feelings aside for the sake of the children.

Please allow me to share two incidents regarding children from broken homes with whom I am currently involved. With the help of *Hashem*, I am confident that the first child will mature into a self-confident, well-adjusted young woman. I hope that I am wrong, but I do not share that optimism about the teenager in the second story.

Aviva is a bright 6-year old girl attending first grade in a local Bais Yaakov. Her parents divorced four years ago. Aviva lives with her mother, and spends most weekends with her father, who lives in the same community. Her parents are both very involved in her chinuch and secular education, even attending Parent-Teacher Conferences together. Recently, Aviva went through a difficult week when she was quite rude to her mother. Her mother's response was to call her ex-husband and discuss the matter with him. Twenty minutes later, the doorbell rang. It was Aviva's father. He took Aviva for a drive and discussed with her the importance of treating her mother with respect. Throughout the following week, Aviva's parents conversed nightly with each other to monitor the situation.

Yossie's parents divorced three years ago. It was a messy divorce, with endless litigation about joint assets, custody, and visitation. Yossie's father threatened to withhold a get until he would receive favorable conditions in the asset distribution. Yossie, then 13 years old, and his three siblings were made to appear before a judge to respond to highly personal questions about their relationship with the two parents.

This past Yom Kippur was not on the father's court-mandated visitation schedule. (All nine days of Succos were.) Yossie's father asked his ex-wife for permission to spend Yom Kippur locally (he has since moved away from his former community) and meet Yossie in shul for the davening so that "Yossie shouldn't be the only child in shul without a father." This reasonable request was refused, and he was informed that any attempt on his part to follow through on this plan would result in court action.

*Yossie is currently a bitter young man who has been in several yeshivos in the past two years. He spends his nights "hanging out," and has a strained relationship with **both** his parents.*

It is of paramount importance that in the event of a divorce, all parties design a plan of action that will provide the children with the most pleasant home environment that is possible under the circumstances.

THE THIRD PARTNER

For the record, I do not think that children from orphaned homes are included in the high-risk category. Aside from the pledge of the *Ribbono Shel Olam* — the *Av Hayesomim* — to watch over his special children, anecdotal evidence would indicate that the overwhelming majority of *yesomim* grow to become well-adjusted, very often outstanding, young men and women. Tempered in the crucible of the pain and loneliness of losing a parent, they often outgrow the inevitable "Why me?" phase, mature earlier than their peers, are more sensitive human beings, and become exceptional spouses and parents, having learned at an early age to appreciate life to its fullest. And, they usually develop an incredibly close relationship with the surviving parent who raised and nurtured them under such difficult circumstances.

GENUINE WARMTH

*I*t is interesting to note that the initial attraction to *Yiddishkeit* for many *chozrei b'teshuvah* is not a beautiful *d'var Torah* or deep thoughts of *hashkafah*, but rather their participation in the warm atmosphere of a Jewish family sitting around the *Shabbos* table. Throughout the generations, our homes have always been the anchor in our lives and one of the primary sources of the transmission of our *Mesorah* to future generations. And it is in our homes — down in the trenches — that our generation's *milchemes hayeitzer* (battle for spiritual survival) is being fought.

May the *Ribbono Shel Olam* grant us the wisdom and *siyata diShmaya* to create the type of home life for our children that will inculcate them with Torah values and prepare them to transmit our timeless *Mesorah* to yet another generation.

Chapter Six

SHOULD WE KEEP OUR AT-RISK CHILD AT HOME?

DEAR RABBI HOROWITZ:

We have six children ranging in age from a married daughter of 22 to a son of 8 years old. Things are well with us, B'H, regarding shalom bayis, parnassah, and other areas of our lives.

We are writing to you regarding our 17-year-old son, who is a (very) at-risk teenager. We have been supporting him with testing, tutors, etc. throughout his school years, but nothing seemed to have worked. He's been in several schools since ninth grade, has dropped out and is currently working full-time. We have an excellent relationship with him; he is respectful and does not violate Shabbos/kashrus in front of our family members. But he is, at this point in his life, completely non-observant.

Our dilemma is with regard to his four siblings still in our home. We are terribly worried that they will pick up his habits and lifestyle. We have so many questions:

1) Should we ask him to leave our home, as many of our friends tell us to do? We don't think that is a good idea.

2) How can we allow him to remain in our home and turn his back on all we hold dear?

3) What do we tell our other children? They all know what is really going on to some degree, depending on their age.

We are so torn over this decision. Adding to the confusion is all the diverse and conflicting advice we are being given by people. We are hearing many different voices. Some say, "Be firm." Others say, "Be flexible." Some say, "Give him an ultimatum." Yet others say, "Always keep the lines of communication open." What should we do?

We would be most grateful for your advice. Thank you very much.

Names Withheld

RABBI HOROWITZ RESPONDS:

The first thing that struck me about your letter was your obvious confusion because of the conflicting advice you are receiving from many different people. I hear this frequently from so many parents who are in your excruciating situation. I hope that this column will help you sort things out and not add to the glut of information.

Before I get into the details, I'd like to inform you that after reading your letter I have a strong hunch that you are doing exactly what you ought to be doing. Why do I say that? You write that you have an excellent relationship with your son; trust me, if your relationship survived his rocky school experience and crisis of faith, you should be giving guidance to parents yourselves.

While there is little I can do to completely allay your fears about your other children picking up your son's rebellious behaviors, I can tell you that in my 25 years of dealing with at-risk kids and their families, I have rarely found that a child went off the *derech* because he/she followed a sibling who strayed from *Yiddishkeit*. I think that what often skews the data and leads people to believe that off the *derech* is a contagious condition are situations where there are significant flaws in the family dynamics that are left unaddressed and uncorrected, despite the fact that a child has previously exhibited rebellious signs.

Now for some answers to your questions:

1) I am usually reluctant to give advice to people I do not know, but there does not seem to be any reason for you to even consider asking him to leave your home. I would respond differently if you had mentioned that he was self-destructing (substance abuse, for example), or was undermining your authority or the quality of life at home, or if you felt that there was a clear and present danger of another child going off the *derech*. But none of these seem to apply, so I don't think sending him away is even a subject for discussion in your situation.

To parents who are experiencing one or more of these three conditions I mentioned in the previous paragraph, I usually recommend that they first go for counseling to try and improve things, and to gain a clearer understanding of the issues at hand. Then, armed with that information, parents should visit their Rav in order to present their request for guidance. I do not think parents should make *dinei nefashos* (life-or-death) decisions regarding sending a child away from home without both of those components: medical and rabbinic advice.

2) Please review my chapter "Leaving the Door Open" for guidance that I received from one of our *gedolim*, who told a father in your situation to inform his child that he ought not feel disenfranchised from *Hashem's* Torah and its eternal lessons just because he does not fully understand it all at the young age of 17 – for growing close to *Hashem* and comprehending His Torah is a lifelong mission. You, as parents, can be most helpful in reframing your son's "no" to a "not yet."

3) What should you tell your other children? I have a simple answer for you. Tell your children that you love them all unconditionally — always and forever. And that means giving each one, including the at-risk child, the attention that is needed at that moment. Explain to your other children that at this juncture in his life, your 17-year-old needs understanding and acceptance above all, and as difficult as this is, you are committed to provide it. This is the most honest and beautiful thing that you can tell your children – indicating that they would also receive the same measure of unconditional love, time, and acceptance from you if they had a crisis of any sort in their lives. Tell them that they, too, should love their brother unconditionally and not withdraw their emotional support for him due to his eroding faith in *Hashem*.

I cannot predict the future, but I can assure you that the best chance you have that your son will find his way back to *Hashem* is to follow the *darchei noam* approach I suggested. The bedrock of your unconditional love will hopefully provide the platform upon which your son can gently and slowly build, and return to Torah and mitzvos.

I usually do not mix my *parashah* and parenting columns, but I will make this exception and inform you of a profound *dvar Torah* that my dear friend Reb Pinchas Gershon (P.G.) Waxman of Lakewood shared with me.

The *Gemara* (*Shabbos* 89b) relates that when the Jews will stray from the path of Torah and mitzvos, Hashem will inform our *Avos* (Patriarchs) that their children have sinned. Avraham and Yaakov Avinu will respond that they ought to be punished for their misdeeds. Yitzchak, on the other hand, will implore the *Ribbono Shel Olam*, "Are they (*Klal Yisrael*) only *my* children? Are they not *Your* children as well?" The *Gemara* notes that Yitzchak will continue to plead until *Hashem* spares *Klal Yisrael* from destruction.

This is quite difficult to understand. Why was Yitzchak Avinu the only one of the *Avos* who was able to defend the Jews at that time? This is all the more puzzling as Yitzchak was noted for his attribute of *gevurah* (firmness), so he should have been the last one of the *Avos* to successfully defend his children.

One possible explanation is that of all the *Avos*, Yitzchak was in a unique position to advocate for the Jews since he kept his son Esav in his house despite Esav's numerous sins. He sent his beloved son Yaakov (not Esav) away when Esav wanted to kill him; and furthermore, when Esav's wives worshiped idols and Yitzchak was becoming blind from the smoke of their incense, he still did not ask Esav to leave home.

Therefore, Yitzchak was able to plead with *Hashem*. "I kept and loved my child Esav despite his significant flaws; You too, should [keep and] forgive Your children."

I do not profess to understand *Hashem's* workings, but perhaps when the Jewish people are one day in need of forgiveness, the two of you, and all others who unconditionally love and believe in their at-risk sons and daughters, will emulate Yitzchak Avinu and advocate for all of *Hashem's* children.

(Reb Pinchas Gershon later found a similar thought in the writings of the chassidic Rebbe, Reb Meir of Premishlan. For further discussion of this matter, see Rashi, Yirmiyahu 31,15; Ein Yaakov, Panim Meirim Yayeitzei, Emes L'Yaakov Toldos 27,40.)

Chapter Seven

LEAVING THE DOOR OPEN

*D*ue to my involvement with at-risk teens, I am often contacted by parents seeking advice about guiding their children through turbulent phases in their lives. Some of the questions posed are rather straightforward in nature, while others require the wisdom of Shlomo Hamelech. Fortunately, several of our leading *gedolim* graciously permit me to seek their guidance and benefit from their Torah wisdom.

One such incident occurred several years ago when the father of a 17-year-old *bachur* asked me how to react to a conversation that his son had had with him the previous day. It seems that the young man, who was a very high achiever in yeshivah, informed his father that he was undergoing a crisis of faith and at that point in his life had significant questions regarding the fundamentals of *Yiddishkeit* that his rebbei'im had taught him. The *bachur* was still externally observant but he felt that he was simply going through the motions. Moreover, he did not think that he would be able to continue his life as a *ben Torah* much longer without resolution of his faith-based questions.

My initial response was to compliment him on being an excellent parent, as his son was clearly comfortable discussing this loaded subject with him – something not all teenage boys would do. I then informed him that although I had some thoughts on how he ought to respond, I felt that I ought to seek *da'as Torah* myself.

I placed a call to one of our leading *gedolim*, explained the dilemma faced by the boy's father and asked him for guidance in developing an appropriate response. The *rosh yeshivah* waited only a short moment before answering with the timeless words of David Hamelech. יְמֵי שְׁנוֹתֵינוּ בָהֶם שִׁבְעִים שָׁנָה – the days of our lives are [merely] seventy years (*Tehillim* 90a). He explained that David Hamelech was expressing the notion that our life's mission is to spend our finite time in this world doing our very best to understand all of *Hashem's* Torah and live our lives according to its principles.

On a pragmatic level, the *rosh yeshivah* suggested that the *bachur* consult with a *kiruv* professional who would be more familiar with issues of *hashkafah* than would be most *rebbei'im* in mainstream yeshivos. Equally as important, he said, was that the father should inform his son that he ought not feel disenfranchised from *Hashem's* Torah and its eternal lessons just because he does not fully understand it all at the young age of 17 – for growing close to *Hashem* and comprehending His Torah is a lifelong mission.

Simply put, the *rosh yeshivah* wanted the *bachur* to reframe his thinking regarding his *emunah* status from "maybe" or "no" to "not yet." Why? Because a "no" mind-set leads to frustration and a sense of despair that usually results in a downward spiral. A "not yet" attitude, on the other hand, conveys the duality of the realization that one is far from the goal of perfection, while at the same time sending a profound message of perpetual growth while striving to reach a lofty objective.

Many solutions to the at-risk-teen phenomenon are costly, complicated, and difficult to implement. But an enhanced level of tolerance costs nothing and can make a very meaningful difference to a child or teen who is in the "not yet" phase. A caustic comment or a judgmental look from one of "us" can telegraph an unintended message to a vulnerable child that he or she is not welcome in our community; while a kind and encouraging word can convey love, acceptance, respect, and faith in his/her future.

A distinguished rabbi recently approached me and asked me to share a personal experience of his with my readers. Nearly 30 years ago, a young man who came from a very distinguished Orthodox family and who was no longer observant approached him in *shul* on Yom Kippur. This individual informed the rabbi that he felt drawn to attend Yom Kippur davening despite his nonreligious status, but that he was troubled by a nagging question. Somewhere in the recesses of his mind, he remembered hearing from his *rebbei'im* that if one repents out of sincere love for *Hashem*, all his previous sins are transformed to merits.

"Come on, Rabbi," he asked. "Do you really believe that? How is it possible for *Hashem* to consider everything that I have done in the past few years as mitzvos? Do you have any idea how many terrible things I did? How can God ever accept me back? I might believe that *Hashem* could wipe my slate clean, but how could the things I have done ever be considered mitzvos?"

The rabbi was quiet for a long moment, not really knowing how to respond. He then softly informed the young man that one day in the future he might wish to take all the mistakes and experiences of his youthful rebellion and utilize them to assist others who find themselves in similar predicaments. Thanks to his past, he would better understand how to help others. "When that happens," said the rabbi, "your actions in the past will all become *zechusim* – for you, and for the children whose lives you will save."

The rabbi informed me that this young man eventually devoted his life to helping wayward teens, and is currently heading a program in Eretz Yisrael that has, over the past two decades, enabled hundreds of at-risk teens to regain their footing and become proud, productive members of our Torah community.

Chapter Eight

ELEVATOR PITCH

*A*n *elevator pitch* or *elevator speech* is a short overview of an idea for a product or service. The name reflects the fact that a short, crisp presentation can be effectively delivered in the time span of an elevator ride: about 30 seconds. Entrepreneurs seeking funding for their ventures and marketers looking to sell their products all work to perfect their *elevator pitch*, since the rule of thumb in marketing and sales is that if one cannot make a compelling case to sell one's product or idea in 30 seconds or less, then one hasn't got anything saleable. The *elevator pitch* has become such a critical component of business culture that countless books have been written on the subject and people attend multi-day workshops designed to help develop, craft, and perfect the ideal *elevator pitch*.

Well, I recently witnessed a remarkably effective *elevator pitch* for a Torah lifestyle in … an elevator of all places!

It was Thursday evening and I was visiting a family member who was on the eighth floor of Maimonides Hospital in the Boro Park section of Brooklyn, New York. In the lobby, I boarded the elevator, which was filled with individuals representing a wide range of ethnic and religious backgrounds. One floor up, several people disembarked from the elevator, and two women walked in: an Oriental nurse and an Orthodox woman, the latter a regular volunteer for the local Bikur Cholim. They were in midconversation, with the nurse finishing a description of her plans for Saturday and Sunday. She then turned to the volunteer and asked her, "So what are you doing this weekend?"

The *frum* woman responded with a 100-watt smile and said, "You know, the nicest thing about being Jewish is our Shabbos. For 25 hours, I turn off my cell phone and e-mail. I just enjoy my husband and children, unwind from the week, and try my best to get closer to G-d." The elevator bell rang for her floor and she exited with the nurse she was conversing with. As she walked out, all of us still on the elevator heard her say to her friend, "You can't imagine how much I look forward to Shabbos all week long."

Silence reigned as we rode upward, but it was quite evident that her words had a powerful impact on all those who heard them. In fact, as the only Orthodox Jew remaining in the elevator, I got a few meaningful glances from the other passengers who were obviously mulling over her words.

My friends, that was about as close to a perfect *elevator pitch* for a Torah lifestyle as I have ever seen or heard. Judging from the looks of my fellow elevator-riders, they were envious of the serenity in the woman's voice as she described her Shabbos experience.

If I may take a page from the *elevator pitch* philosophy, my 30-second response to the question of how to effectively deal with the colossal challenges of the Internet and technology would be that we need to improve the quality of our home life. I would venture to say that if we all had tranquil, peaceful homes infused with *shalom bayis* and *simchas hachaim,* the teen drop-out rate would dramatically decrease and we would be far better equipped to deal with

"Wal-Mart" in the months and years ahead. If our children had feelings for Shabbos similar to those of the woman in the elevator, fewer of them would be populating hangouts and abusing substances.

About eight years ago, a *frum* woman living in Yerushalayim sent me a fascinating dissertation that she had prepared for her postgraduate schooling. In it, she explored her theory that there was a direct correlation between how children enjoyed Shabbos in their homes and how connected they felt to *Hashem.*

Over the course of a school year, she interviewed many dozens of girls who were attending seminaries in her community. As part of the study, she asked each of them to describe their home environments during four time periods — Thursday nights, Friday afternoons, Friday nights, and Shabbos mornings. Many of the girls wrote beautiful comments about how relaxed they felt coming home Thursday nights and smelling Shabbos cooking, how peaceful their homes were on Shabbos, and how much they enjoyed the time spent with their siblings and parents. Sadly, a significant number wrote about the stress and anxiety, about tense Shabbos tables filled with discord and negative energy. The woman conducting the survey then asked these same girls to assess their own feelings about *Yiddishkeit* and *Hashem.*

Analysis of the data collected in her study revealed a stunning correlation between the two components of her study. Those with positive Shabbos experiences were more spiritual and observed mitzvos more regularly. Most of them reported that they planned to send their children to the types of schools they attended and wanted to parent their children the way they were raised. Conversely, the girls who reported stress at home were far more disconnected spiritually and more inclined to reject the values of their parents. And these patterns were consistent, regardless of whether a girl was attending a *chareidi* or a modern Orthodox seminary.

So while our attention may be focused on the external challenges we face in today's environment, we may be better served by turning inward and improving the quality of our home lives. In fact, I strongly feel that … sorry, it's the eighth floor. Gotta go!

Chapter Nine

RISING ABOVE

*A*nyone who is fortunate enough to be able to engage in conversation with a brilliant thinker like Rabbi Dr. Abraham J. Twerski is bound to develop a fresh perspective on things. A discussion I had with Dr. Twerski a number of years ago about the topic of at-risk teens most certainly fits that pattern. He remarked to me that most people are looking for solutions to the teens-at-risk crisis by focusing on those who dropped out of our school system. "Wouldn't it be interesting," he asked, "to focus some of our energy and attention on those who achieve success despite experiencing some of these risk factors?"

Dr. Twerski mentioned that he would be most interested in conducting a research study on children who grew up under conditions that seemed to point to future "at-risk" behavior but who became outstanding adults nonetheless. "Imagine how things would improve," he wondered aloud, "if we could replicate the successes of these individuals in young men and women who are currently confronted with similar challenges during their adolescent years?"

Well, Dr. Twerski, if you ever read these lines and are still interested in that project, it would be my pleasure to introduce you to two ordinary, extraordinary people who would be ideal candidates for your study: Rabbi Herschel Meisels and Mrs. Sarah Rivkah Kohn.

Rabbi Herschel Meisels, a descendant of a long chain of chassidic rabbis, is a soft-spoken, unassuming individual with an easy smile and an engaging personality. At the age of 5, he was diagnosed with juvenile (type 1) diabetes. One can only imagine the challenges he faced managing the medical ramifications of his diabetes and dealing with the social stigma of growing up in a close-knit community with a condition that requires constant monitoring. One does not need any imagination, however, to analyze how Rabbi Meisels harnessed the energy created by the challenges of his formative years. He started "Friends With Diabetes,"[1] to help Jewish diabetic children/teens – and their parents. There are currently more than 2,000 children on the mailing list for the organization's bimonthly publications and hundreds of children, couples, and parents attend seminars and Shabbatons each year.

Mrs. Sarah Rivkah Kohn was raised in Monsey and currently resides in Brooklyn, where she is a homemaker and mother of a 1-year-old daughter. Her mother passed away while she was in her early teenage years and she often thought how helpful it would have been for her to have had the comfort of a network of girls who, too, were coping with the searing pain and loneliness of losing a parent. Several years ago, Mrs. Kohn actualized her dream and published a newsletter called LINKS,[2] geared to provide support, practical advice, and a sense of camaraderie to *frum*, orphaned girls. Sadly her mailing list continues to grow exponentially and currently has more than 300 members.

---

1. For more information on "Friends With Diabetes," call 845-352-7532 or e-mail rabbimeisels@friendswithdiabetes.org

2. For more information on LINKS, call 718-851-4778 or e-mail olamhabo@verizon.net

Recently, I got a firsthand look at the incredible work of these two individuals when I participated in Shabbaton retreats conducted by "Friends of Diabetes" and "LINKS." In both instances, I was asked to inspire others and walked away uplifted myself.

The "Friends of Diabetes" event was entirely upbeat, where more than 70 boys had a grand time together. In fact, the only time I realized that it was a gathering of diabetics was during the Motza'ei *Shabbos* festivities, when I noticed that quite a few boys seemed to be checking their cell phones and sending text messages incessantly. It was only when I looked closer that I noticed that those devices were in fact blood sugar monitors that the boys were scanning and calibrating. I suspect that they were, in some way, celebrating the fact that they could whip out those gadgets and tinker with them in a public setting without being subjected to curious glances and uncomfortable questions.

The LINKS Shabbaton, on the other hand, was a blend of Yom Kippur, Simchas Torah, and Tishah B'av. More than 50 teenage girls spent two full days together laughing, crying, talking, and bonding. There were art-and-crafts and aerobics activities, as well as sessions on understanding the grieving process and open forums where the young ladies were able to seek the counsel of trained adults as they struggle to comprehend the incomprehensible. When I left my hotel room at 5 o'clock Shabbos morning, I found that 30 of the 50 girls had been up all night and were sitting in the lobby deeply engrossed in conversations – not even noticing my presence.

Of the entire gamut of emotions that I experienced over that LINKS Shabbos, one poignant moment stood out above all the others. It was during a session that I conducted on the subject of blended families. I fielded a broad range of questions from dealing with stepparents and stepsiblings to how, when – and if – to "allow" the single parent to remarry. A young lady asked a heartrending question. She mentioned that a *rebbetzin* told her during the *shivah* mourning period that the *neshamah* of her departed mother would be reunited with her father and family members in Gan Eden. She wanted to know what would happen if she did as I suggested and gave her blessing for her father to remarry. Would her mother's *neshamah* then be excluded from their family? And if that was the case, was she being disloyal to her mother by "allowing" her father to remarry?

All in all, both of these gatherings left me filled with hope and encouragement. Due to the passion and dedication of Rabbi Meisels and Mrs. Kohn, many hundreds of children are offered resources and services that simply did not exist a generation ago. When my father died before my 4th birthday, my mother and her children — my sister, brother, and I — had to cope in the best way we could. Today, things are thankfully different.

My remarks to both these groups included the suggestion to the youngsters to note the living examples of both organizations' founders, and use the painful experience of their own youthful years to help future generations of *Hashem's* children.

Chapter Ten

DIFFERENT STROKES

PART ONE: UNDERSTANDING YOUR CHILD'S LEARNING PATTERN — AND YOUR OWN

DIFFERENT STROKES ...

*I*magine that a close friend of yours is planning a party and asks you for a detailed weather forecast for the next three days and nights. Assuming that you possess all the information that your friend desires, you could share this knowledge with him in a number of ways:

You could give him all the facts that he needs in narrative form — **in writing** — and hand him a piece of paper that reads: Tuesday will be sunny with a high temperature of 87 and a low of 65; Wednesday will be cloudy with a … etc.

You could present him with the information orally — by **speaking** to him and informing him of the weather situation.

You could show it to him **visually** — by presenting him with a graph of the three days with the high and low temperatures for each day clearly noted. You may decide to dress up the chart by writing the high and low temperatures in red and blue ink, respectively. You could also attach a picture of the sun on clear days and clouds on rainy ones.

Which is the best format to use in order to present this information to your friend? Well, that question is difficult for me to answer, since I do not know the learning-retention style of your friend. But if you wish to be of true help to your friend, it is important for you to know that there are distinctly diverse learning patterns. For the record, there are more than these three learning patterns, but that is beyond the scope of this series of articles.

… FOR DIFFERENT FOLKS

*S*ome people learn best by reading. They get distracted when people are talking and they like to learn and study in a quiet setting. You may have had a friend with this learning profile. When you learned a difficult piece of *Gemara* with him, you may have been surprised — or perhaps insulted — when he asked you to refrain from talking for a few minutes while he read the *Gemara* several times and quietly absorbed the information. Perhaps that was the case because you didn't understand that although you acquire knowledge by listening to people speak, your friend finds it distracting. While you get energized by crowds, noises, and high-tempo environments and may do your best studying for tests with music blasting in the background, your friend wonders how you can possibly concentrate with all that ear-shattering noise.

Yet another friend of yours has a remarkably different learning pattern. While he can learn on some level by reading and listening, the best way to his mind is through visual learning. Whatever he sees remains imprinted in his mind almost permanently. He loves graphs and charts, but his eyes glaze over and his mind shuts down while reading lines of text that contain exactly the same information as the visual aid that so stimulates him.

THINKING BACK

*T*hink back to the time that you were leaning *maseches Yevamos* in the *Beis Midrash* in your late teens, and your friends were struggling to understand the complex family ties described in the *Gemara*. You probably didn't realize it then, but those diverse learning styles were on vivid display for all to see.

Some of you concentrated on the *Gemara* and read those lines of text again and again. Others had their *chavrusos* (study partners) read the *Gemara* to them and tried to sort it out that way. At the same time, there were some boys who set pen to paper and began drawing the family trees that the *Gemara* described and came to a better understanding by viewing the diagram that they drew.

UNDERSTANDING YOUR OWN LEARNING PATTERN — AND YOUR CHILD'S

*O*nce you start thinking in these terms, you will begin to understand your own unique learning pattern. More importantly, as you try to help your child succeed in school and life, it may be helpful to think about his or her learning style.

Keep in mind that in my example of the *Beis Midrash* of your late teen years, you and your dissimilar friends were very much in the driver's seat as you learned. You were each able to acquire the *Gemara* according to the style of thinking that works best for you. Not so in many classrooms, where information is sometimes presented in only one or two modalities. And I suggest to you that if your child is receiving information in only one or two of these three methods, he or she may be inadvertently deprived of a significant opportunity for accomplishment in school.

As a supportive parent, you can gain a deeper understanding of these learning patterns and help your child thrive and succeed.

Chapter Eleven

DIFFERENT STROKES

PART TWO: HELPING YOUR CHILD SUCCEED BY PRESENTING LEARNING IN DIVERSE MANNERS

llow me to share an observation with you. I have found that although the visual learning profile follows a continuum — meaning that people have this profile in various degrees — the most extreme examples of visual learners often tend to be the creative-impulsive-restless types. These are the children who will, in all likelihood, become entrepreneurs later in life. They are out-of-the-box thinkers who respond beautifully when stimulated, but get bored easily. They simply do not have the patience to listen to an entire class that is delivered without visual aids nor do they possess the persistence to read the entire *Chumash* or *Gemara* enough times to master it properly. They are the ones who desperately need the visual and diverse learning that will stimulate their minds and senses.

VISUAL IMAGERY

While this column is primarily intended to address parenting matters, I would like to use these lines to appeal to parents and educators alike to use visual imagery during classroom and homework time to help more of our precious children achieve success in school and in life.

With reflection and creative energy, almost any *limud* (subject) or lesson can be taught — or re-taught at home — in diverse ways.

One day, I observed the fourth-grade *rebbi* in our yeshiva, Rabbi Avrohom Chaim Lowi *shlita,* begin his *Chumash* lesson in the creative manner with which he introduces nearly all his *shiurim.* The *talmidim* were all in their seats with their *Chumashim* opened. Without saying a word, Rabbi Lowi walked up one of the aisles and took the hands of three children. Gently holding their three left hands in his right hand, he walked them one at a time to the front of the classroom. They remained standing there, enjoying their moment in the spotlight. *Rebbi* then took three chocolate coins from his desk and motioned for three other boys to join him at the front of the classroom. Each of the boys was given a chocolate coin when they arrived near *Rebbi's* desk.

Rebbi then instructed the *talmidim* to read the *Rashi* on the *pasuk, Ves amo lakach emo* (*Shemos* 14:6), which describes how Pharaoh took (*lakach*) his people to follow the *B'nei Yisrael* to the *Yam Suf. Rashi's* unasked question is how can people, especially such a large group of people, be *taken? Rashi* answers *kocheim bedevarim* — he *took them* with words — encouraged them by offering them the spoils of the Jews. When *Rebbi* read the *pasuk* a few moments later, nearly all the *talmidim* independently anticipated *Rashi's question* — and his answer. Watching this excellent visual introduction (sometimes referred to as an anticipatory set), it was obvious that although this type of visual aid is the lifeline for the learning of some of the *talmidim, all* of the *talmidim* utilized the demonstration to prepare for what they were about to learn.

This entire visual image event took no more than three minutes of class time — and greatly enhanced the learning of all the *talmidim*. In fact, when I privately asked several of the children after the *shiur* to relate the day's *Chumash* to me, each of the boys I spoke to made reference to the living parable that *Rebbi* enacted for their benefit.

Chapter Twelve

DIFFERENT STROKES

PART THREE:
TEACHING GEMARA VISUALLY

HELPING YOUR CHILD SUCCEED BY PRESENTING LEARNING IN DIVERSE MANNERS

*N*owhere is the visual presentation of learning more important than in the area of teaching *Gemara* — primarily in the first few years of its introduction. It is during these middle-school grades that students are introduced to so many different challenges **at the same time.**

Baruch Hashem, the majority of our *talmidim* make this adjustment quite well. However, many need additional assistance to master this new *limud*. The reason is quite simple. Once the *talmidim* transition from *Mishnah* to *Gemara*, the students, who are in the early phases of adolescence, are at once:

1) beginning to read without *nekudos* (vowels);

2) learning a new language (Aramaic);

3) and perhaps most challenging, using deductive reasoning to follow the track of the *Gemara*.

Even for the *talmidim* who can master the new language and the new reading skills they now need, many find following the line of *sevarah* (reasoning) very challenging.

IM TIMZA LOMAR (IF YOU WILL SAY)

Take the thirteen lines of *Gemara* in *Bava Metziah* 24a, in *Perek Eilu Metzios*, the classical *Gemara* taught in beginner or second-year *Gemara* classes throughout the yeshivah world. The *Gemara* lists a series of five interlinked questions regarding a statement of Rabbi Shimon ben Elazar.

Rabbi Shimon mentioned that one who finds an object in a place frequented by many people may keep it, because the owner who lost it would not expect to ever retrieve that article from such a well-traveled location.

The *Gemara* then poses five questions in sequence. Here are the first three:

1) Was Rabbi Shimon stating his halachah regarding a city where a majority of the people were non-Jews, but in a city with mostly Jews he would not permit the finder to keep it?

2) And, if Rabbi Shimon would maintain that the finder could keep it even in a city that has a majority of Jews, do the *Rabbanan* (a term often used in *Gemara* for a "majority" of sages who disagree with a single sage) agree with him?

3) And, if the *Rabbanan* disagree with Rabbi Shimon, would their disagreement extend to all cities or only to cities populated by a majority of Jews?

FINDING THIS DIFFICULT?

*I*f you are finding it difficult to clearly follow the thread of the *Gemara* by reading these words without visual aides, it may be comforting to know that you are not alone. Many adults find this challenging.

All the more so for the beginner *talmid* who is just getting used to Aramaic, with no *nekudos* — often at the same time that his school day has significantly been extended by *minyan* in the morning and a later dismissal in the afternoon. Having taught an eighth-grade "*beis-shiur*" (the weaker class) for 10 out of the 15 years that I had the *zechus* to serve as a *melamed*, I had a firsthand view of the frustration in the eyes of many dozens of bright boys who felt that they were unable to follow the logical flow of the *Gemara*.

INTRODUCING MY TALMIDIM TO LOGICAL FLOW CHARTS

*T*he first time in the school year that I would encounter a *Gemara* of this nature, I would utilize various techniques for training my *talmidim* to commit multistep logical sequences to paper. One of the methods I would employ would be to have my *talmidim* jointly write a script for a group of people who were doing follow-up phone calls for the Yeshivah's Annual Dinner. (A script is a visual chart of a conversation and all possible ways the dialogue will flow. It is usually given to all customer-service employees or telemarketers to help them decide what to say to the customer in a variety of possible scenarios.)

One boy would come up to the board and begin the chart with a "Hello," and get input from his classmates as to the next possible steps of the conversations. He would note the first question that a Dinner phone-squad member would ask: "Did you receive our invitation in the mail?" I would ask my *talmidim* what they would suggest the caller say if the response was "yes," (Ask the next question: "Will you be attending?) and if he or she said, "No" ("Can I send you an invitation in the mail?" or "Can I take your reservation over the phone?").

My *talmidim* loved the exercise and were trained in mapping thoughts and logical sequences on paper. Having acquired this skill early in the year, we were able to map out the logic of the *Gemara* each time we encountered a multistep *shakla v'tarya* (give-and-take of the *Gemara*).

By mapping out the flow of the *Gemara*, *talmidim* (and adults) have a much better chance of grasping the beautiful and timeless *shakla v'tarya* of our great *chachamim*. They, too, can recite with *cheshek* the precious words of, "*Vas fregt Abaye, un, vas enferet Rava*" — once they are given the tools to succeed.

SAMPLE FLOW CHART FOR THE PHONE
SQUAD OF A SCHOOL'S ANNUAL DINNER

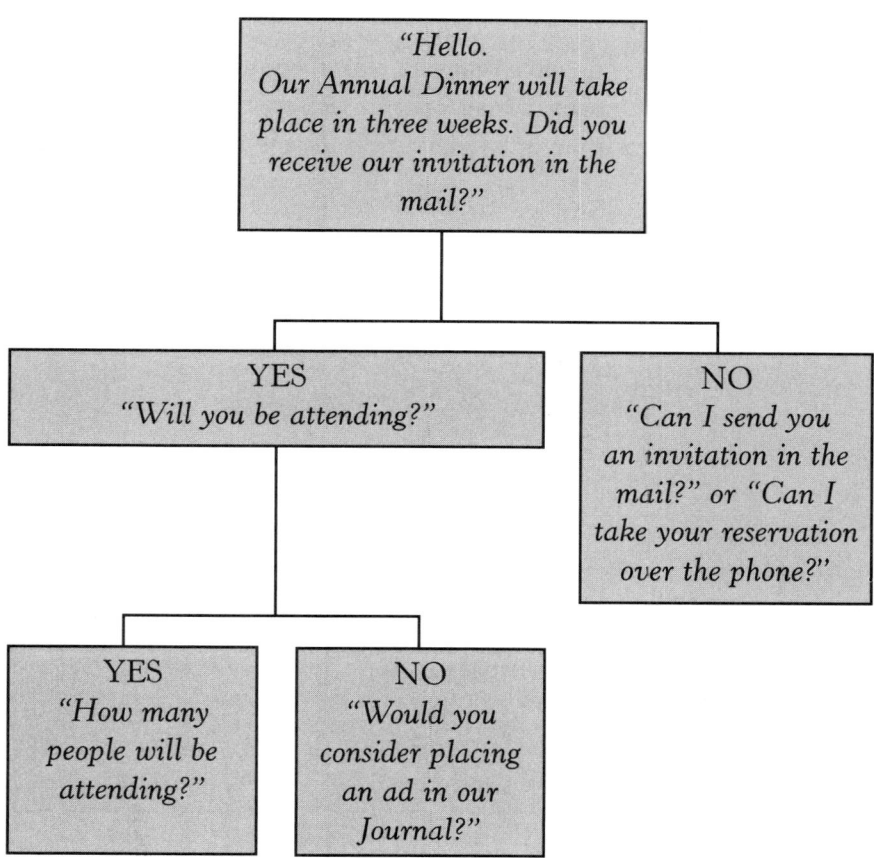

"Hello.
Our Annual Dinner will take
place in three weeks. Did you
receive our invitation in the
mail?"

YES
"Will you be attending?"

NO
"Can I send you
an invitation in the
mail?" or "Can I
take your reservation
over the phone?"

YES
"How many
people will be
attending?"

NO
"Would you
consider placing
an ad in our
Journal?"

FLOW CHART FOR THE *GEMARA* (*BAVA METZIAH* 24A)

*I*ntroduction:
Rabbi Shimon says that one who finds an object in a place frequented by many people may keep it because the owner who lost it would not expect to ever retrieve that article from such a well-traveled location.

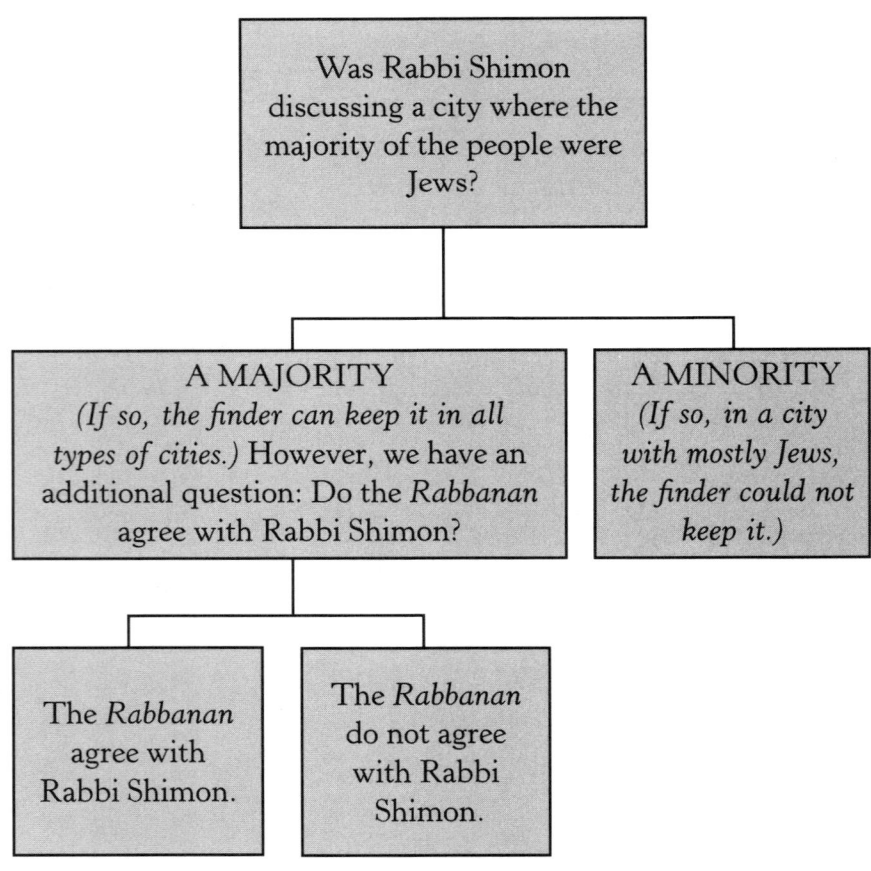

Was Rabbi Shimon discussing a city where the majority of the people were Jews?

A MAJORITY
(If so, the finder can keep it in all types of cities.) However, we have an additional question: Do the *Rabbanan* agree with Rabbi Shimon?

A MINORITY
(If so, in a city with mostly Jews, the finder could not keep it.)

The *Rabbanan* agree with Rabbi Shimon.

The *Rabbanan* do not agree with Rabbi Shimon.

Chapter Thirteen

IT DOESN'T START IN TENTH GRADE

*I*t is rare to find a single "smoking gun" a clearly identifiable cause — to explain why a child regresses from the "inner circle" of successful students to the "outer ring" of uninspired learners, and perhaps even to those who *r'l* sink into the morass of at-risk behaviors. After all, there are a huge range of non-educational factors – parenting and social/emotional issues — that often play a significant role in a child's success in school. Having said that, I think that we would all agree that we have a sacred obligation to reflect upon, and seek the counsel of our *gedolim*, as to the most effective way to educate our children so that they all reach their fullest potential.

While much attention is focused on the teen years, when many at-risk children begin exhibiting symptoms of distress, I strongly feel that in many instances the slide began far earlier, when children failed to acquire the basic skills they desperately need to achieve success. In order to illustrate the point, please permit me to present the following scenario:

Imagine that you received an offer from a generous benefactor to head a group of kollel fellows in learning the writings of Rambam (Maimonides) in their original Arabic over a period of ten years. You would love to take the assignment, but there is one slight problem. You don't understand a word of Arabic. Your prospective donor tells you not to worry. He informs you that he is confident that you will master the language and bring new insight to the timeless works of Rambam.

Assuming that you accepted the offer, how would you go about designing the ten-year program?

Well, there are basically two paths that you could choose. One would be to take the strategic route. You would designate significant blocks of time at the onset to carefully and methodically study the language of Arabic. After all, how could you possibly understand the basic text of Rambam's works, let alone the nuances of his every word, without a thorough understanding of the language?

You would consult with an expert in learning foreign languages. You might be advised to proceed slowly, as learning a foreign tongue is often frustrating – and there is significant danger of "burnout" if you progress too quickly at the beginning of the program. Additionally, you may decide to set a long-term goal of mastery of all the many topics that the Rambam draws on regularly in his writings — *Chumash, Halachah* and all portions of *Nevi'im* and *Kesuvim*. You would look high and low for the best Arabic-English dictionary money could buy and keep it at your side at all times — along with the phone number of an expert translator.

There is a second and far simpler route that you could take: You can simply jump in headlong and begin reading Rambam's classic

Morei Nevuchim (*Guide to the Perplexed*; a very deep and difficult philosophical work) in Arabic the very first day. As far as the language barrier – no big deal! You figure that you will pick up Arabic as you go along. After all, you are a bright fellow and you already speak Hebrew, English, and Yiddish. It can't be difficult to learn another language, can it? You figure that the longer you keep at it, you will just get better and better at Arabic. For good measure, you borrow an Arabic-English dictionary from the local library.

Reading these lines, which of the two programs described above do you think will result in a greater chance for success? The first or the second? The slow-and-steady approach or the ready-or-not-here-I-come one? Who do you think will reach the finish line first — let alone healthy and well adjusted — the tortoise or the hare?

Well, if you think about it, our pre-teen sons are in a very similar situation to that of the fictional program described above. Our sons have a ten-year "fellowship" program, during which we hope that they will master the intricacies and timeless beauty of *Gemora*. However, in order to achieve that objective, they will need to learn to read a new language — Aramaic — without *nekudos* (vowels). The best way to achieve that lofty goal is a question of approach and methodology. What type of program will allow our children to thrive and reach the finish line having mastered, appreciated, and developed a lifelong love for *Gemara* and learning? A slow, skill-based, balanced approach or a hurry-up program that will teach them "a lot" but not that well?

This is not a "new" discussion. Read through the writings of the Maharal and others on this topic and you will discover that they suggested a methodical and systematic approach to mastery of *Tanach* and *Gemara* hundreds of years ago

In these challenging times, when not "making it" in yeshivah translates into squandered childhoods, unrealized potential, and sometimes a complete abandonment of Yiddishkeit, we would do well to make a serious communal *cheshbon hanefesh* (soul-searching) and decide if the *hora'as sha'a* (extenuating circumstances) of the climate nowadays mandates that we slow down the pace a bit and properly prepare our children with the skills they will need to succeed.

Kids don't drop out in 10th grade. They fall behind in the fifth and sixth grades. And they never catch up.

Chapter Fourteen

TRAINING WHEELS

*I*t was a few days after *Rosh Hashanah* 5756 (1995), and we had just arrived home from the hospital after the birth of our youngest child. After we put our older children to bed, my wife and I were enjoying some "quality time" with our baby. At one point, my wife, who has the uncanny ability to read my thoughts, asked me to explain that faraway look in my eyes. I sheepishly admitted that I was calculating how old I would be when the time would come for me to remove the training wheels from Sara's bicycle and run alongside her until she would be able to successfully ride without falling. (I was about forty-two when the training wheels came off, if you must know, and that phase has mercifully passed).

Training wheels are a remarkable invention. Once they are properly affixed to a child's bicycle, he or she only needs them for a short period of time. Once the child acquires better balance and agility on a bicycle, the training wheels are lifted a bit. Then a bit more. Soon, they are removed completely and the child never looks back. You know what they say, "You never forget how to ride a bicycle."

I think that this analogy of bicycle riding and training wheels carries profound lessons for us as we chart a course for the *chinuch* of our precious children in these challenging times. If one takes a few steps back and surveys the overall landscape of how we sometimes educate children, one might be struck by a puzzling dichotomy. We seem to be offering our children a significant array of learning assistance and support after some form of educational failure has occurred. However, very few of these tools are offered to children who are in the critical "training-wheels" phase of their learning experience.

Going back to the bicycle analogy, that would seem to be like having our children start riding their bicycles without the benefit of training wheels, and only providing them to those who have severely injured themselves by repeatedly falling off their bicycles.

Think about it. If a child is falling behind in his/her learning, we place him/her in a remedial program. There, a skill-based educational approach is taken, where children are given more time to acquire the skills they will need to succeed. This phenomenon is even more pronounced in "at-risk-teen" *yeshivos*, where all sorts of educational and motivational techniques are employed to help the young adults appreciate Torah learning. If a grown man finished his years in *yeshivah* without having mastered *Gemara* learning, it is perfectly appropriate — and culturally acceptable — to make use of an Artscroll *Gemara*, replete with *nekudos*, translation, and learning tools, such as charts and diagrams that work so well with visual learners.

I am most certainly not suggesting that we start teaching *Chumash* and *Gemara* to our children using English translation. What I do recommend is that we invest the time to teach children properly in their formative years so that they have the tools to succeed and develop a lifelong love for learning *Hashem's* Torah.

Take the study of *Chumash*, for example. More than ninety percent of all words that appear in *Chumash* are variations of only

270 root words! There are 26 verbs (ex. *yatza, holach*) and 38 nouns (ex. *lechem, makom*) that appear in *Chumash* more than 500 times each! If we were to give children a proper rudimentary understanding of the language, *Lashon Hakodesh* — teach them the *shoroshim* and *shimushim* (root words, prefix, suffix, etc.) — before or as soon as they start learning *Chumash*, we would be providing them with the educational "training wheels" they need to succeed.

This is not a "new" concept. Even a casual reading of Rashi's timeless commentary on *Chumash* reveals how critical *Lashon Hakodesh* skills are in mastering *Chumash*. It is impossible to understand Rashi's commentary, let along his nuances, without these skills.

Ironically, many or most girls' schools have been teaching *Chumash* using the skill-based approach for decades. However, many or most mainstream boys' school do not employ these methods. Schools for at-risk boys do, as do the resource-room programs in mainstream schools – but not the "regular" classes.

I believe that these critical skills are even more essential in the learning of *Gemara*, where Aramaic is introduced, *nekudos* are removed, and the lengthy nature of *Gemara* logic comes into play. A few missed or misunderstood words at the opening lines of a class can result in many days of frustration and underachievement, until a new topic is introduced.

In the broader scheme of things, it is only a minor investment of time in the formative years of the education of our precious children that can provide them with these critical educational training wheels. In today's challenging climate, we must do all we can to teach them slowly, carefully, and thoroughly while they are young and eager to learn.

The road they will need to ride is far more dangerous than ours was. The downhill slopes are much steeper and the boulders encroaching on the sides of the path are getting larger every day.

Chapter Fifteen
LIFE SKILLS

I think that a clear delineation ought to be made between the study of secular studies and the acquisition of life skills. Studying Shakespeare or learning physics (both of which, for the record, were part of the curriculum when I attended Mesivta Torah Vodaas in the 1970's) could be fairly represented as secular studies. But learning to be articulate in one's native tongue and being able to express one's thoughts clearly in writing are extremely important life skills. Included in this description are learning the requisite math skills needed to calculate interest rates on a credit card or to balance a checkbook. I maintain that teaching a child these life skills are incumbent on every father nowadays, as they are prerequisites to the obligation of a parent to teach a child a trade (*Kiddushin* 29-30).

Let us for a moment set aside the majority of our children who will seek employment in the business world, as they will most certainly need these skills to feed their families and pay the tuitions of their children. The brutal fact is that the vast majority of those entering the workforce lacking language/math/computer skills will be forced to take lower-paying jobs. But even – or perhaps especially – those who will be inspired to pursue a career in the rabbinate, *chinuch* or *kiruv* will desperately need these tools to succeed. Sure, one can point to individuals who have been successful in these fields without these skill sets. But they are the exceptions rather than the rule – just as there are those who are less than literate and who have become wildly successful in business. Having interviewed prospective *rebbei'im* for teaching positions, and counseled hundreds of sincere *yungeleit* looking for post-*kollel* jobs over the years, I can tell you firsthand how critical these skills are for those wishing to enter *chinuch* or *rabbanus.*

One would be hard pressed to maintain that these skills are a barrier to Torah greatness. The Rambam, who served as a court physician, wrote beautifully in Arabic, and Rashi was quite the expert in Old French. Rabbi Isaac Don Abarbanel served as the finance minister of Spain, and Rabbi Meir Shapiro was a member of the Polish Parliament. And while many of the European *gedolim* who came to America following the Holocaust did not develop a command of the English language late in life, they were all fluent in the native tongue of their original host countries. Read the biographies of my *rebbi*, Rav Avrohom Pam, and his *rebbi*, Rabbi Shraga Feivel Mendlowitz. Both of these Torah giants took the time to learn English properly in order to be able to communicate with their *talmidim* effectively.

It is also historically inaccurate to suggest that our *gedolim* were opposed to providing our children with a solid general studies education. Rabbis Moshe Feinstein, Yaakov Kamenetsky, Gedalia Schorr, Avrohom Pam, Mordechai Gifter *z'tl* all presided over *mesivtas* which had excellent general studies programs.

Enhanced language and writing skills enable a Torah scholar to expand his sphere of influence wider and wider, like ripples in a pond. If one needs an example of the exponential power of effective writing to spread Torah learning, one need look no further than the

Torah revolution generated by the proliferation of quality English *sefarim* over the past 30 years that is perhaps unparalleled in our glorious history.

Rabbi Moshe Sherer, the legendary president of Agudath Israel, understood the importance of having *yeshivah bachurim* acquire these skills. Over a period of many years, he took time each week from his busy schedule to teach a voluntary homiletics (public speaking) class which I had the good fortune to attend for an entire winter while in my late teens. Rabbi Sherer often told us that we ought to view this skill building as an integral component of our training to become the disseminators of Torah to the next generation.

When I speak to my *talmidim* about the importance of applying themselves to their general studies classes, I often quote the words of our *rebbi*, Rav Avrohom Pam. In his classic Friday *shmuessen*, he would often tell us that regardless of our professions later in life, we would all need to become teachers of Torah eventually. He explained that when *Mashiach* will come, *Klal Yisrael* would need each and every one of us to teach Torah to our brothers and sisters who did not have the privilege to study its halachos and lessons during their formative years.

Helping our children acquire the skills to learn and teach Torah in an articulate and erudite manner is a goal we should all strive to achieve.

Chapter Sixteen

SKILLS FOR LIFE

TEACHING OUR CHILDREN TO BECOME INDEPENDENT LEARNERS

here are basically two ways to teach *Chumash* to beginners (the same concept applies to *Gemara*, albeit with modifications for *Gemara* terms and phraseology). One approach is to teach by memory/rote. In this method, when a "new" *pasuk* (verse) is taught, each word is translated. The students then repeat the *pasuk* and translate the words in the timeless singsong tune passed down through the generations. This is primarily a memory-based exercise, where the children retain the words they are taught – all the while building a growing vocabulary of words that they have already memorized.

The other approach is a skill-based one. This method is based on the notion that children ought to first (or simultaneously) be taught the basic structure of *lashon hakodesh*. They are introduced to the meaning and usage of the main *shorashim* (root words) and *shimushim* (prefixes and suffixes) that are used to conjugate the root words.

You probably know by now that I am a strong proponent of the slow-and-steady skill-based method of learning. I feel that this fulfills the proverbial concept of "teaching a child how to fish." Investing the time to teach our sons and daughters the skills that they will need to succeed is the greatest gift we can offer them. A skill-based approach to *chinuch* results in independent learners who have the tools to enjoy the exploration of the various *limudim* (subjects) in which they engage.

Rote learning, on the other hand, requires an enormous amount of memorization and only works well with children to whom committing large amounts of material to memory comes very easily. Additionally, the rote process is often difficult for creative children, for visual learners, and for restless/distractible children. Finally, it leaves many children – and adults – with a great volume of knowledge, but not necessarily the ability to connect the dots and form an understanding of the Hebrew language that will allow them to open a *Chumash* and read a *Ramban* with ease.

Why is that so? Well, please permit me to share an analogy with you. Think of the last time that you attended a family wedding. There, you may have been introduced to a distant relative for the umpteenth time. Somewhere in the recesses of your mind, you know that he is related to you somehow. The only problem is that you are just not quite sure how that connection is made. Is he your father's brother's cousin through marriage? Or is he your father's cousin's brother-in-law? It may be exceedingly frustrating for you; somehow you just can't seem to get it right no matter how hard you concentrate and/or how many times you repeat the information to yourself.

Well, my dear reader, that is what it feels like to a child (or adult) who has learned *Chumash* by rote and who is now trying to understand the connection between *vayomer, vatomer, amarti, leimor, imri, vayomru, amru, amar, amarnu* … you get the picture. The individual knows that these words are interlinked somehow, since all are derived from the root word *amar*, but he or she doesn't quite know exactly how the Lego pieces of Hebrew language click together. So, rather than memorizing several hundred *shorashim*, the rote learner must memorize many thousands of the cousins, uncles, and aunts of these root words.

Some are under the impression that children will pick up the language as they continue to learn and memorize more words. But that is not the way complex languages are taught. Just think back to your school days and all those color-coded posters in your classrooms charting the creation of blended words – **"can + not = cannot or can't."** Those charts, the lessons you were taught, and all the exercises in your grammar workbooks gave you a mental map of how those words were formed. If this is the case in the English language, it is all the more so with *lashon hakodesh* where root words, and the almost infinite numbers of permutations they form by means of the addition of the various prefixes and suffixes, make up the very core of language training.

This sounds quite logical, doesn't it? So why aren't all our children[1] learning this way? As I see things, there are three main reasons: 1) The notion that the teaching of skills is somehow a departure from our *mesorah*, 2) the thinking that investing the time to teach skills will result in diminished quality and/or quantity of learning, and 3) relentless, unbearable pressure from parents (that's you) on school principals to "cover ground," or face the alternative of having their schools relegated to second-tier oblivion.

There must be a better way to educate our children.

---

1. It is important to note that nearly all our girls already learn this way, as do the boys in remedial classes around the world.

Chapter Seventeen

CONSTRUCTIVE CRITICISM:

A DISH BEST SERVED WARM

*A*s parents we have a sacred obligation to be teachers and guides—*morei derech*—for our children. We are mandated by our Torah to teach them right from wrong, to train them to conduct themselves properly, to show them the light.

It is not in our children's best interest—nor is it in our own best interest—to become their friends. That is, we should be *friendly*, but we do them no favor if we allow them to do as they please. At times, it is grueling being a parent and having to guide a child who doesn't particularly want direction. It's much easier in the short term to allow misdeeds to go unnoticed. But in the long term, you face an increased risk of raising unruly children whose moral compass may be underdeveloped.

It is of utmost importance to give clear guidelines and direction to your children. Setting limits for your children and establishing boundaries are crucial for the success of your children – at home and in school. Having a set of house rules and expectations for appropriate behavior, dress, and language are all critical parts of the mission statement of any family, subjects that will be addressed in later columns.

And while it is true that our children will learn more from what we do than from what we say, guidance in the form of constructive criticism is an integral component of parenting.

Our challenge is to couch the criticism in a constructive way so that:

1) Our children internalize the important messages that we wish to convey to them.

2) The end result is improvement and a desire to grow, not increased friction and tension that may harm our relationship with our beloved children.

Rabbi Yaakov Kamenetsky *z'tl* offered an insightful commentary on delivering proper *tochachah* (constructive criticism). He pointed out that in the initial encounter between Yaakov Avinu and the shepherds of Lavan, Yaakov addressed the shepherds as "My brothers"—"*Achai, mei'ayin atem* — My brothers, from where do you come?" (*Bereishis* 29:4).

Rabbi Kamenetsky explained that Yaakov's sense of honesty and integrity was offended by the fact that the shepherds had finished their workday early and were, in effect, being dishonest by cheating their employer out of a full day's work. Yaakov wanted to rebuke them — and, in fact, did so later in the conversation — but decided to begin with words of brotherhood and friendship.

There is a famous expression, "Revenge is a dish best served cold." And although revenge is forbidden by our Torah, I'd like to paraphrase that idiom and say, "Criticism is a dish best served warm."

If you have a message to deliver, make sure that the message is delivered calmly and, most importantly, with love. If you cannot do that, then wait until you can. If your child feels that you're just venting your anger and that you are disgusted with him or her, then no matter how articulate you are, what comes across instead is: "Mommy or Daddy doesn't like me."

It's very important that the message of *tochachah* does not get blurred by the static of anger. And, of course, this is very difficult to do when there's a tumult and emotions are flying high. That is when it is best to delay saying anything.

One Friday morning, I received a phone call from a person whose son was suspended for a full week from an out-of-town yeshivah for a series of infractions. The boy was flying home for the week, and his father wanted to know what to say to his son when he picked him up at the airport.

I said, "I think you should tell him that you're disappointed by what he did, but that you love him unconditionally, and that you'll always be there for him."

He was surprised. "That's it?"

"You should also tell him that you're terribly upset that this happened, but you want to make believe he came home for an unscheduled visit. And that you'll discuss this important matter with him after Shabbos."

"Nothing else, after what he did?" the father asked me, taken aback.

So I told him, "Look, he's expecting you to attack him as soon as he gets off that plane. He is going to be highly defensive and is not likely to listen to whatever you say. You are probably just going to get into a bitter argument with him. But if you say nothing now, he will be very relieved and grateful. And when you speak with him after Shabbos, you will have a meaningful conversation with him, because he will be listening to you at that time. Keep in mind that you will have a much better chance to make a positive impact when he is calm and grateful for your patience."

Chapter Eighteen

CONSTRUCTIVE CRITICISM:

A POSITIVE VIEW OF YOUR CRITICISM

To begin with, you, as the parent, need to have a positive view of your guidance, since your viewpoint is subconsciously communicated to your children. Think of *tochachah* as a gift that you are giving your child. But bear in mind that it will be in all likelihood an unwanted gift — at least temporarily — because few people take pleasure in listening to criticism. Your goal, therefore, is to deliver this gift in such a way that it is accepted, even if it is not appreciated at that time.

Many years ago, I heard Rabbi Shlome Wolbe *z'tl* describe children as little adults. As he put it, *"Kinderlach zenen kleineh menschen."* Although they are small, children still have feelings just as we adults do. And just as we would be, they are hurt if we present our criticism in a nonconstructive manner. Therefore, make sure that your gift of *tochachah*—even if less than pleasant—is delivered in a positive manner.

One summer I was teaching a group of 15-year-old students at camp. As I went through the roster on the first day of class and I called out the boys' first and last names, one student corrected me in a harsh tone of voice, "My name is not Shloime. It is Scott."

I was taken aback by his words. I wanted to say to him, *Not that there is anything wrong with the name Scott, but what do you find offensive about Shloime? What's wrong with Shlomo? You have a beautiful Hebrew name. Why not use it?* I was also quite upset by the tone of his voice. But I stopped myself and thought, *This is the first day of class. I have eight weeks to learn with this child. I would like to teach him Torah, middos, and how to be a proper Jew. He doesn't know me yet, so whatever message I give him today will probably be lost. So this is not the time for tochachah.* In all honesty, this child was not my *talmid* at that time; he was just a child sitting in my classroom. I felt that I would do a better job getting my message across after I had developed a relationship with him.

I did get the message across later in the summer, but on that first day, it clearly was not the time.

Sometimes, delayed criticism is more effective, but it takes a lot of self-discipline not to give into a knee-jerk reaction. When we see something wrong, we feel the urge to respond immediately. And without a doubt, it is good to correct wrongful behavior on the spot — if we can do so in the right way. But there are times when our closeness to the situation is such that we're not in the best position to deal with the problem immediately. In such a situation, it might be wise to say nothing, or to say, "I am upset by what you did, and for this very reason I don't want to discuss it right now. We need to sit down and talk about it, and we'll do it when we have had the time to think calmly about what happened."

I personally learned this lesson from a renowned *talmid chacham* of the previous generation. I witnessed him do something that made an unforgettable impression on me when I myself was a teenager.

A child in a sleep-away camp was sent home for a serious in-fraction. The Rav called the boy's father and told him that he was putting his son on the bus, so he should arrange to pick him up. With the father listening over the phone, the Rav then delivered a very strong rebuke to the boy. Then he gave him a blessing and told him to leave. But, as soon as the camper was out of his office, the Rav called the father back and told him, "Your son is devastated. I gave him all the bitter medicine he needs. You don't need to give him any more tochachah. What you need to do now is to embrace this child and help him to get on the right road again."

Chapter Nineteen

CONSTRUCTIVE CRITICISM:

AVOIDING HURTFUL LABELS

The *Vilna Gaon z'tl* says that the best *tochachah* —the only valid *tochachah*—is focused *l'haba*, on future improvement. That is, we should not dwell on what happened in the past, but be clear what kind of behavior we would like to see in the future. That's a positive message. "Yesterday you may have done something wrong. Here's what I would like to see from you tomorrow."

When disciplining your child, try to frame the discussion in terms of consequences as opposed to punishments. Framing the consequences as logical outcomes of improper behavior makes for less resentment on the part of your child. It will also, in all likelihood, result in long-term improvement.

A consequence can loosely be defined as an outcome of one's poor behavior. There is a direct correlation between the misdeed and its consequence. Your child can learn positive, long-term lessons about avoiding these types of consequences in the future by exhibiting self-control and avoiding the behavior that resulted in the consequence.

A consequence of a child leaving a messy room would be to have him or her clean it up during a time that he or she would rather be out with friends. A punishment would be not allowing him or her to go to the park later in the day after the room has been cleaned. The punishment in this case has nothing to do with the misdeed.

Obviously punishments are in order when misdeeds are done, and there are many types of poor behavior that cannot be presented as consequences. But creatively thinking in terms of outcomes and consequences will hopefully enable your child to grow from the unpleasant experience of being on the receiving end of your *tochachah*.

Several years ago, I was invited by the owner of a summer camp to conduct a staff-development lecture with his counselors. I addressed several topics — among them the subject of constructive criticism. I began by asking for a volunteer willing to describe the last time he criticized a camper.

It was quiet for a few moments. Then, a very charming young man raised his hand. "I admonished one of my campers today in front of the whole bunk," he proudly stated.

I asked him to describe what happened.

So, in his self-confident, teenage manner, he began, "Well, I caught him going through my things in my cubby. He was reading a private letter of mine. And ... you know ... I told him what he had to hear."

Before he launched into any further details, I immediately told him that unless he was an angel, I was quite confident that he had not handled this situation well. I explained to him that he was simply too close to the situation. The offense was not something that he'd observed being done to someone else — it had been perpetrated against him personally. And he didn't have time to carefully formulate a response.

Sure enough, his response had been that he had told his camper — in the presence of the entire bunk — "You're a thief, and I'm never going to trust you again." Moreover, he informed the child, "I'm going to tell your *rebbi* about this."

I was quiet for a moment. Then, I asked him, "Can you think of a time when an adult-figure in your life called you a less-than-flattering name? What was the label that the person gave you? What do you think that person was trying to convey to you? And finally, how effective was his criticism?"

The young man related how he had been admonished for his (admittedly) inappropriate dress on a school day, and how a member of the faculty used a label with negative connotations when delivering the *tochachah*. Of course, he shared with his peers that the *tochachah* was ineffective, and upon reflection, he mentioned that he was clearly resentful that he had been given an insulting label.

I suggested to the camp counselor that instead of calling the boy a thief, another way to handle the incident would have been to say to him — privately, without humiliating him in front of his peers — "You're a nice kid, and I'm very disappointed that a boy like you would invade my privacy and take something belonging to me." We then spent the better part of an hour discussing techniques for delivering effective and meaningful *tochachah*.

Chapter Twenty

CONSTRUCTIVE CRITICISM:

A CHANCE TO MAKE AMENDS

*W*hen giving criticism to our children, it is important to offer them an opportunity to do *teshuvah*—a way to make amends, to right the wrong. It is important to tell our children what they did wrong, but it is equally important to tell them how they may make it right.

Many years ago, at the age of 22, I was a rookie rebbi, teaching a challenging class of eighth graders. With the help of Hashem, things worked out well, but it was, shall we say, an interesting year.

At Purim time when the students were a bit restless and in a mischievous mood, I received a complaint from the proprietor of a local fish store whose business was just around the corner from the yeshivah. It seemed that two of my students had rolled a smoke bomb into his store just as he was in the midst of preparing orders for Shabbos. It was a disaster. The store was filled with smoke, and all the customers came running out. His entire day was disrupted.

From his description, I was able to identify the perpetrators. I called them out of class and spoke to them. I said, "Look gentlemen, it seems to me that you two guys were involved in last week's activity at the fish store."

To their credit, they didn't deny it.

I said, "Look, boys, you need to accept responsibility for what you've done. Here are your choices: you can get punished or you can try to make amends. If you choose punishment, you will probably get suspended or expelled from school."

They pleaded and begged me for a way to make amends. I suggested that they "walk a mile" in the shoes of the store owner— that is, go into the fish store for an hour that Friday afternoon, put on a pair of gloves, and prepare orders for Shabbos.

They looked at me stupefied. "Rebbi, come on!"

I said, "I don't think that you have any idea how hard this man works to provide for his family. Working there for an hour will give you perspective and allow you to make amends for what you have done. If you don't want to do what I am suggesting, that's fine. I'll just play this one by the book."

They talked it over and decided that my approach was far better than punishment. I explained to them once again that after they had done the work for an hour, they would have a better understanding of the damage they had caused by disrupting the man's hard day at work, and that would be a giant step on the path to their teshuvah.

After school was over that day, I took them to the store and introduced them to the owner. We made an appointment for Friday afternoon. As it turned out, by the time Friday came, *many of the kids in the school knew about our arrangement and begun playfully ridiculing them. My talmidim begged me not to humiliate them, now that it had become public knowledge. They were even getting orders from their classmates for fresh fish!*

So, I had rachmanus (mercy) on them. I told them that instead of working, they could buy the fish-store owner a gift from their own money. I insisted that they devote some time over the next few weeks to earning some money and using it to pay for their gift to the man they had wronged. They bought him a $25 gold pen-and-pencil set, and inscribed a card to him. The man was satisfied and impressed with the sincerity of the boys.

The point was, of course, that there had to be a significant consequence for what these boys had done, and I do think that this resolution offered them an opportunity to right the wrong.

While the vast majority of misdeeds do not require creative solutions, our emphasis as parents should be on constructive consequences – with an opportunity for sincere *teshuvah*.

Chapter Twenty-One

CONSTRUCTIVE CRITICISM:

SETTING A PERSONAL EXAMPLE

*R*av Samson Raphael Hirsch, *z'tl*, offers an insightful point regarding the well-known statement of our Sages: *Kasheit atzmecha v'achar kach kasheit acherim* — Criticize yourself [first] and after that [you can] criticize others (*Sanhedrin* 18a). The phrase is traditionally understood to mean that one should reflect upon one's actions and self-evaluate before having the temerity to criticize others.

Rav Hirsch says that the first time that the term *kasheit* is used in this phrase, it is related to the Aramaic word *kushta*, meaning *truth* (as in *Alma Dikshot* — the world of truth; a reference to the

World to Come). In other words, be truthful with yourself before rebuking others.

Effective *tochachah* only occurs in an environment of intellectual honesty. Rav Hirsch implores us to look at ourselves honestly before we address the faults of others. We transmit best to others that which we believe ourselves.

Many years ago, when I served as an eighth-grade rebbi, I had the pleasure of teaching a grandson of Rav Shimon Schwab *z'tl*. At the bar mitzvah of my *talmid,* Rav Schwab *z'tl* related a beautiful *dvar Torah* on the topic of parents as role models, which he later published in his *sefer Ma'ayan Hasho'eivah.* He used an incident that took place in the months preceding the birth of Shimshon Hagibor (Samson) to illustrate his point.

The prophet (*Shoftim* 13:3) relates that an angel came to Shimshon's mother and told her that she was going to have a special child, who would be a *nazir,* meaning that for the boy's entire life he would live as an ascetic: he would not be able to drink wine, cut his hair, nor come in contact with the dead.

When the woman related this incredible episode to her husband, Manoach, he prayed (ibid v.8): יָבוֹא נָא עוֹד אֵלֵינוּ וְיוֹרֵנוּ מַה נַּעֲשֶׂה לַנַּעַר הַיּוּלָּד — Dear G-d, please send the angel to us again, and teach us what to do with this special child who will soon be born." The angel then appeared to them a second time and told the father (ibid. v.13), "מִכֹּל אֲשֶׁר אָמַרְתִּי אֶל הָאִשָּׁה תִּשָּׁמֵר — Whatever I told your wife (the first time that I appeared), that is what you should do." The angel then shared with Manoach some rules about *nezirus.* Upon hearing these instructions, Manoach expressed his gratitude to *Hashem* for the additional directives.

Rav Schwab asked, "What additional guidance did he receive during the second visit of the angel? Didn't Manoach trust his wife? Why did he need the angel to repeat his instructions? And if, in fact, Manoach needed assistance regarding the laws pertaining to a *nazir,* could he not have read them directly from the Torah?"

Rav Schwab offered a fascinating interpretation of Manoach's request and of the response of the angel. He explained that Manoach was troubled by the fact that he was being asked to raise a child with a set of halachos that he would not subscribe to. He asked Hashem, "How can I raise my child as a *nazir* when I myself will be drinking wine? How can I possibly be *mechanech* my son when I am following a different set of rules?"

During the second visit of the angel, said Rav Schwab, the angel told Manoach, that he, Manoach, should also assume the role of a *nazir*. מִכֹּל אֲשֶׁר אָמַרְתִּי אֶל הָאִשָּׁה תִּשָּׁמֵר — *You* should do all that I told the woman." *Hashem* agreed that Manoach would have great difficulty raising a child with different standards than those he followed, and therefore instructed him to take upon himself all the stringencies of a *nazir*.

Setting a personal example is the most effective manner of transmitting our beautiful tradition and value system to our children.

Chapter Twenty-Two

CONSTRUCTIVE CRITICISM:

COMMUNICATING UNDERSTANDING

When we attempt to offer constructive criticism to our children, we are often met with, "You just don't understand what I'm going through." You know; our children do have a point. We don't really understand, because the drives and temptations of a child — or a teenager — are not the same as those of an adult. As much as we think that we empathize with our children, it may be difficult for us to remember what it was like when we were young.

Indeed, the Rambam addressed this issue in *Hilchos Teshuvah* (2:1). He states that complete repentance occurs when a person experiences the same set of circumstances as those that prevailed during the time that he or she committed the original transgression — and finds the fortitude to withstand the moral trial the second time around. However, if the person transgressed as a young man and in midlife faces the same situation without faltering, the *Rambam* says this is *not* an indication of complete *teshuvah*. The reason is that the temptations of a young person and a middle-aged man are very different, so the situation cannot be described as the same.

Since it is so hard for us to imagine ourselves in our children's situation, it is important, when delivering *tochachah*, to communicate to our children that we are stretching ourselves to understand their reality – trying to see the world through their eyes.

A *talmid* of *Mori V'Rabi*, Rabbi Gedalia Schorr, *z'tl*, the renowned *rosh yeshivah* of Torah Vodaas, related to me that when he was in his 30's and very involved in his professional career, Rav Schorr let him know that he needed to make time to study Torah as well. How Rav Schorr did this is an apt illustration of communicating understanding even while delivering *tochachah*.

Rav Schorr began the conversation by asking the man about his personal and professional life, affording him the opportunity to describe with pride how his medical practice was progressing. Then Rav Schorr complimented him. He said, "I'm very proud of you. I see that you didn't become a machine. I can understand that when you're making hundreds of dollars an hour, it's very tempting to take on more and more patients in order to expand your practice. But I see you don't do that. You make plenty of time for yourself and for your family, and I'm impressed that you have your priorities in order. I imagine that this must be a tremendous test for you, and I am pleased that you have passed it very well."

The man was extremely flattered. He thanked Rav Schorr for his insight and for his kind words. And then my *rosh yeshivah* looked at him and said with a smile, "So, do you have time to learn Torah at least six hours per day?"

In relating the story to me, the man said, "What an incredible message of *tochachah*! My *rebbi* wanted me to know that he understood exactly what I was going through. I know that he didn't have to deal with the same issues in his professional life as I did in mine. And yet he communicated to me that **he** understood **me**."

It's no coincidence that this man finished Shas several times in the 30 years since this conversation took place.

Our *tochachah* has a much greater impact if, when delivering it, we can communicate to our children that we have some measure — albeit an imperfect one — of understanding of their reality. When we do so, it is much more likely that our children will listen to what we have to say with receptive ears.

The renowned author and lecturer, Reb Avi Shulman, recently delivered an in-service workshop titled "Effective Classroom Discipline" to the *rebbei'im* of Yeshiva Darchei Noam, where I serve as Dean.

During his presentation, he vividly described how impressed he was by the sensitivity of his dentist. When Mr. Shulman was having a cavity filled, he was informed by his dentist that a shot of Novocain would be given to him to dull the pain of the drilling and filling. Mr. Shulman related how he watched with interest as his dentist held the vial of Novocain cupped in both his hands for a few moments before injecting it into Mr. Shulman's mouth. He explained to Mr. Shulman that in addition to the sting of the shot, patients often feel discomfort when the room-temperature Novocain is injected in their 98.6 degree bodies. He therefore warms the Novocain in his hands before injecting it.

What a powerful message to educators and parents! We have a sacred obligation to guide and direct our children. At the same time, we must keep in mind the importance of projecting warmth and protecting the dignity of our children when we deliver these important messages. Warm the Novocain. Warm the Novocain!

Chapter Twenty-Three

CONSTRUCTIVE CRITICISM:

WHEN THE LABEL STICKS

SEEKING MODERATION

*W*e learn from the Torah that effective criticism emphasizes misdeeds without attaching labels and passing judgment on the person. When Yaakov Avinu criticized the actions of Shimon and Levi, for example, he was careful to direct his *tochachah* only to their anger (*Bereishis* 49:7, see Rashi and other commentaries). He did not insult *them*. He directed his criticism toward their *actions*.

Labeling children negatively can often result in their internalizing that message, with quite disastrous consequences.

Several summers ago a young man came to see me. He was very well dressed and was driving an expensive car. He sat down and I asked him a casual question, "How are things going at home?" His answer was anything but casual. "You know, Rabbi, I don't get along with my parents. It's my father. He's so different than I am. He is driven, and I am chilled out. He's up at 5 o'clock in the morning; he works all day and learns Torah at night. Besides that, he's involved in many *tzedakah* projects."

"And you are?" I asked.

"Me? I'm a lazy, good-for-nothing bum."

That was his self-image. Obviously, he had not arrived at it himself; it was a label that someone, perhaps his father, had inadvertently given him. And, sadly, it stuck. What had happened?

It is interesting to note that character tendencies, especially in their extreme manifestations, sometimes skip a generation – and for good reason.

Take the example of a woman who is meticulously neat at home. She spends inordinate amounts of time tidying up and making her home immaculate. Often, her daughter grows up and says to herself, *Mom has no life. All she does is walk around making beds all day. When I get older and have my own home, I'm not going to do that. I'm going to spend time with my kids. I'm going to have a cup of coffee in the morning. I'll relax, and if the house isn't beautiful, we'll get it cleaned up in time for Shabbos.* So she grows up and has a messy house.

Now, *her* daughter, growing up in a messy house and going to visit friends who have beautiful, clean homes, says to herself, *I'm not doing this in my home. I'm going to have a clean house.*

The young man whose father was so driven was a perfect example of this pattern. This young man's father grew up poverty stricken, and he made up his mind that he was going to work hard until he achieved his financial goals. His son, on the other hand, grew up in relative wealth. So why did he need to wake up early in the morning? His father, however, was understandably upset and frustrated by his son's lack of focus. The words he spoke to his son were an outpouring of that frustration, "Wake up already, you lazy, good-for-nothing bum."

The young man heard it for years while his father was trying to wake him in the morning. Unfortunately, he internalized it to such an extent that he used it when introducing himself to me. His father meant well. He was trying to get a message across; he was trying to teach his son *zerizus:* to get up and do something with his life. This is a laudable goal, but the message that was heard was anything but a positive one.

Chapter Twenty-Four

CONSTRUCTIVE CRITICISM:

SOME FINAL THOUGHTS

I would like to end this eight part series with an unforgettable story from my great *rebbi*. This is culled from an article that I wrote about Rabbi Avrohom Pam *z'tl* shortly after his passing.

Our great and humble *rebbi* taught three generations of *talmidim* how to deliver *tochachah* with *darchei noam* (pleasantness), by his personal example of *middos* and *derech eretz*.

A LIFETIME OF TEACHING MIDDOS BY EXAMPLE

*W*hen reflecting upon the life of our great *rebbi, Hagaon Harav* Pam *z'tl*, the encounter of the prophet Eliyahu with *Hashem* (*Melachim* 1; Chapter 19) comes to mind.

The prophet relates how Eliyahu was told to stand at a mountain and wait for the presence of *Hashem* to appear. A great, powerful wind blew by him, followed by an earthquake *(ra'ash)*, and then a fire. The *Navi* mentions that these cataclysmic forces were merely the precursor of *Hashem's* presence. And then *Hashem* appeared to Eliyahu in a *"kol demamah dakah* – a still, soft sound" (ibid. v. 12).

Our *rebbi's* manner of teaching and guiding us was always one of a *kol demamah dakah*, but the power and passion of his eloquent, soft-spoken words and the indelible impression of observing his refined character still resound in our ears and hearts.

Perhaps my most everlasting impression of *Rav* Pam *z'tl* was the time some 25 years ago, when he walked into the *Beis HaMedrash* for Shachris. A 10-year-old child had inadvertently taken our *rebbi's* seat, which was in middle of the *shul*, not at the *"mizrach* wall" (a position of honor at the front of the synagogue). As Rav Pam entered, wearing his *tallis* and *tefillin*, several young men went over to the child to remove him from their *rebbi's* seat. Too late. Rav Pam called the boy back. He moved his *tallis* bag to one side of the table and shared his two-person *shtender* with the 10-year-old child. This was the *chinuch* that we received from our *rebbi*. No *ra'ash*, no raging fire, only the *kol demamah dakah* of dignity for the Torah and man.

Before my first speech on the topic of at-risk teens (at the Torah Umesorah Convention in May 1996), I visited Rav Pam, and asked him for his insights and guidance. He was silent for several moments. Then he told me a story. A 65-year-old man had recently approached him at a wedding and thanked him for treating him with dignity and respect when he was a teenager in Yeshiva Torah Vodaas more than five decades earlier. Rav Pam was proctoring an examination, and he observed this young man reading someone else's paper during the test. Fully expecting to have his paper confiscated for "cheating" and to be sent out of the room, this young man was startled when Rav Pam leaned over to him and whispered, "If you are having trouble reading a question, please ask me for help. I will be more than glad to read it for you." (This story is all the more remarkable when taking in consideration Rav Pam's lifelong abhorrence for all things dishonest.) My *rebbi* informed me that the middle-aged man told him that he was struggling in yeshivah at that time, and Rav Pam's trust in him was a turning point in his life. With tears in his eyes, Rav Pam said, "Reb Yakov, imagine how things might have turned out if I had reacted severely?"

Rav Pam then offered his original explanation as to the reason that our sages compared educators to stars. He said that the light of the stars does not reach us on Earth until several years after it was emitted. He encouraged us to remember that we should not become frustrated when we invest our love and devotion into our students but do not see instant results. With the passage of time, the light we now shine upon them will illuminate their lives.

Chapter Twenty-Five

THE PLAN

AN OPEN LETTER TO YESHIVAH BACHURIM

*M*y dear *yeshiva bachurim*,
    Please allow me to share some thoughts with you my dear *yeshiva bachurim*, *Klal Yisrael's* great treasure. After all, you are our future: the husbands of our daughters, the fathers of our grandchildren, the *roshei yeshivah*, *rebbei'im*, and lay leaders who will teach and lead the coming generation. You are now entering a very exciting and challenging period of your lives. During the coming years, you will, with the help of Hashem, crystallize your value systems and search for life partners. You will begin building your own homes, creating a legacy for your children and grandchildren.

Our generation, children of prewar European parents and/or Holocaust survivors, grew up in a dramatically different environment than yours. Our parents came to America and built new lives for themselves and their children. But, as well as they have done, and some have done remarkably well, they never truly felt in sync with American culture. All of them had seen hunger and poverty — real hunger and real poverty. When my parents got married, people who were poor didn't drive old, run-down cars and take inexpensive Chol HaMoed trips. Poor people starved.

I think it is important that you understand one of the most fundamental differences between your generation and mine. You see, by mid-adolescence we had to have a plan. We were asked by our parents, usually in grade 10 or 11, how we planned to support ourselves and our families and what our dreams and goals were. Our parents had rock-solid *bitachon* that enabled them to survive unspeakable tragedy, and they believed with every fiber of their being that *Der Aibeshter vet helfin* — G-d will help. They believed that G-d would help them, that *Hashem Yisbarach* would support their endeavors and bring them to successful fruition. What complicated the equation for thousands of us *yeshivah bachurim* in the 60's and 70's was that virtually all our parents had an almost reverent respect for higher education (here read college). Having been robbed of the opportunity to compete for well-paying white-collar jobs due to the language barrier and the childhood that has been cruelly stolen from them, many of them had no choice but to work very hard at manual, blue-collar jobs in order to provide for their families. In their day, the ticket of admission to a financially secure vocation, career or profession was often a college education. Perhaps many of them overvalued a college education. Perhaps the downside of attending college was less real or less evident than it is today. But that mind-set was the reality among the vast majority of our parents.

And so, as my friends and I passed through our late teens, there was almost no home that was not filled with long, passionate sessions with our parents about what was referred to as *"tachlis"* as in — *"Vus vet zine a tachlis mit deer?"* — What will become of you?" Tears were shed on both sides. *Mamorei Chazal* were quoted (mostly on our side) as we pleaded our case to be allowed just one more year of uninterrupted yeshivah study … and then another year … and yet another. But at no time during the many discussions was there any thought of presenting no plan at all.

The trial of fire that we had to endure to pursue full-time learning made us stronger *B'nei Torah*. We searched our souls, consulted with our *Roshei HaYeshivah*, and discussed these issues with our parents. We embraced each block of hard-fought-for time as the treasure that it was.

Things have changed considerably in the past generation. In virtually all "black-hat" yeshivos, it is certainly the norm, *Baruch Hashem*, for boys like you to learn full time until their wedding and perhaps a year or two beyond that. But at the same time that we rejoice in this monumental accomplishment, this should not discourage you from developing your master plan while you are still in your late teens. Search your soul, discuss this with your parents, and seek the counsel of your *Rosh HaYeshivah*. Call it a *cheshbon hanefesh* or call it strategic planning, but regardless of what you call it, just do it! Go into this process with the understanding that your plan will, in all likelihood, change — not once, but perhaps several times over the next decade. Just remember, an amended plan is a lot better than no plan at all.

A good place to start is to set clear, practical goals for your *limudim*. Read the biography of my great *rebbi*, Rav Avrohom Pam *z'tl*. While in his late teens, he decided to dedicate a two-year period of his life to master all of *Shulchan Aruch*. Then, he single-mindedly pursued this colossal goal until it was accomplished.

A plan is a dream with a deadline. It is the embodiment of *sof ma'aseh b'machshavah techilah* — a beginning with the end in mind. Living your life with a plan is like walking one mile to catch a bus, knowing that it will leave in 20 minutes. You stride with purpose and clarity. Living without a plan is taking that same walk with two hours on your hands. In this case, you are much more likely to meander, or worse yet, get distracted to the point that you miss the bus altogether. The difference between having a plan and not having one is like comparing putting together a jigsaw puzzle with or without the picture on the box to guide you. You might be able to complete the puzzle without that picture, but it is so much easier when you have it there.

Mastering a *mesechta* of *Gemara* needs a plan. Reflect upon your goals and targets for the *mesechta*, and ask yourself some questions. Are you striving for mastery of *bekius* or *iyun* — or both? Are you looking to retain the *yediyos ba'al peh* (information by heart)? Which *Rishonim* (commentaries) will you be learning? How many *dafim* (pages) would you like to learn — by which target date?

Ask your *rebbi* or *rosh yeshivah* to help you develop your personalized learning plan that will enhance your strong points and strengthen your areas of weakness. You may wish to add focus and self-evaluation to your own *limudim* (studies) by writing a summary of each *perek* (chapter) of *Gemara* you have learned or by taking some of the excellent tests created by Mifal HaShas or the Dirshu Kollel.

The next step is to start developing a plan for your future life. Going into *chinuch* is a plan. Going into *rabbanus* is a plan. Striving to become a *rosh yeshivah* is a plan. Continuing to learn is a plan. Becoming a carpenter, an accountant, or a businessman is a plan. But having no plan at all will dramatically increase the likelihood of your leading a floundering and unfulfilled life both in *ruchniyus* and in *gashmiyus*. Once you decide what you want to do, think long and hard about what tools you will need to succeed at this vocation, and get started on developing and honing those skills — today!

Every one of these vocations needs a detailed, multiyear plan to master your profession. Take *chinuch*, for example. If at age 17 or 19, you feel that you have a future in *chinuch*, by all means pursue it. Create your plan — and get started on implementing it ASAP! Give a *shiur* in your summer camp or tutor a weaker *talmid* in your yeshivah. (I decided to enter *chinuch* after teaching a learning group in a summer camp at age 17.)

But don't stop there. Think of the other skills you will need to succeed in *chinuch*: public speaking, writing skills, *lashon ha-kodesh,* and computer graphics. All of these skills will be enormously helpful to you in your quest for *chinuch* excellence and will impede your success if you don't master them. So, get to work. Volunteer to write and edit your yeshivah's newsletter. Deliver a *d'var Torah* in public whenever you can. Spend a summer in Torah Umesorah's Seed Program. Prepare well for your *chaburah,* and, *b'ezras Hashem,* it will be the first link in the glorious chain of your own *harbatzas haTorah.*

Allow me to share with you an observation of mine — one that has, in my opinion, great ramifications for you. Very often, a couple will consult with me regarding a decision that they need to make regarding their son who is currently in *shanah beis or gimmel* (The second or third post-high school year). They and their son agreed that he would learn full-time for a predetermined time after high school. It is now 6 or 12 months after the "deadline." Their son, begging for more time, pleads, "But Ma, I just started really getting into learning." The *Rosh Yeshivah* echoes the sentiment during discussions with the boy's parents. Coincidence? Of course not! Surely the maturity that comes with the passage of time and an acquired appreciation for the virtual Gan Eden of learning Torah *lishmah* makes the third year generally more productive than the first.

There is, however, another factor that makes the last year most productive: the simple fact that it is the last year. Any arbitrary deadline gets your adrenaline running and forces you to crank up your productivity several notches. There are 105 days between January 1 and April 15. With all those days to choose from, more than 25 percent of Americans file their taxes on the day of the deadline: April 15!

Please don't wait for the last year or two to fully appreciate the historically unprecedented opportunity that members of your generation have to devote yourselves completely to learning *mitoch harchavas hada'as.* Spending some time in your mid-to-late teens doing some serious planning for your future life will help you become more focused and productive long before the final year or months arrive.

Another thing that has dramatically changed over the past generation or two is the size, *b'li ayin hara*, of the largest post-high school *yeshivos* and *Kollelim*. Walking into a *Beis Midrash* that has thousands of *bachurim* and *kollel yungerleit* learning Torah is an awe-inspiring experience, but it is of utmost importance that you find a personal *rebbi* within that yeshivah to nurture a long-lasting relationship. *Asei l'cha rav* is an obligation on you, the *talmid*. You will have so many critical, highly personal decisions to make over the next few years — and beyond. Please see to it that you afford yourself the important opportunity to discuss these matters with your *rebbi*, and seek his guidance.

My dear *chaverim*, at this stage, your lives are virtually a blank page. You need to believe that with the help of *Hashem*, you can achieve your dreams and aspirations. So many of the underachieving kids I deal with honestly don't appreciate the gift of life and subsequently squander the precious days, months, and even years of their youth. Embrace life! Unwrap every day as the gift that it is, and live life to the fullest.

(Rabbi) Yakov Horowitz

Chapter Twenty-Six

LIFE-CYCLE SUPPORT FOR THE *BA'AL TESHUVAH* FAMILY

*O*ver the past several decades, tens of thousands of previously unaffiliated Jews have become *ba'alei teshuvah* through the outstanding work of *kiruv* organizations and outreach professionals. Numerous yeshivos in Eretz Yisrael and around the world have implemented programs designed to better appeal to the prospective *ba'al teshuvah*. These programs have all delivered spectacular results; indeed, a veritable *teshuvah* revolution. It is one of the remarkable success stories of the past half-century.

The vast majority of *ba'al teshuvah* programs and *ba'al teshuvah*-oriented institutions, however, focus on the beginning of the *ba'al teshuvah* life cycle: transforming the unaffiliated Jew into a *ben* or *bas Torah*. There is very little "life cycle support" for the *ba'al teshuvah* who has been Torah-observant for 10 or more years, and who is now raising a family – with adolescent or *shidduch*-age children. Those who are fortunate to have attended a well-grounded *ba'al teshuvah* yeshivah and who continue to live in that community generally have the long-term assistance and support they so desperately need. Others are able to find a local *rav* or *rebbetzin* with whom they can bond and develop that special relationship that enables them to receive guidance and direction. But even those couples are but one relocation away from dissolving the lifesaving rabbinical support that is critical to the stability of their family – possibly leaving them with little guidance and direction. Worse yet, they may come to rely on the advice of well-meaning individuals who have little or no experience in guiding *ba'alei teshuvah*.

Effective *ba'al teshuvah* institutions and programs have perfected the art of finding and bringing out the *pintele Yid* in aspiring *b'nei* and *b'nos Torah*. They have the skill and experience to know exactly which blend of rational reasoning and faith-based *hashkafah* should be presented to potential *ba'alei teshuvah* to open their minds and their hearts to accepting a Torah-based lifestyle. These institutions are experts in guiding prospective *ba'alei teshuvah* to adopt the behavioral changes of a Torah lifestyle in slow and careful increments. On the other hand, many well-meaning individuals simply don't have these critical guidance skills.[1]

---

1. I vividly recall spending some time 10 years ago with the talented and dedicated faculty members of Ohr Somayach of Monsey discussing the progress of a young *ba'al teshuvah* with whose progress I had become involved. Over the course of several meetings and phone conversations, I respectfully, but forcefully, disagreed with the recommendations they made. Thankfully, I had the good sense to follow their advice, against my better judgment. With the benefit of hindsight, they were 100 percent correct in their assessment.

Happily, many new *ba'alei teshuvah* are able to make the leap from a secular to a Torah-based lifestyle successfully *at the time*. To this set of new Torah Jews, the Torah-observant community has been increasingly accepting and nurturing over the past 20 years. These individuals are usually single and in their early-to-mid-20's. Often, their *Rosh Yeshivah* is able to help them find their mate and see them to the *chuppah*. If not, they are able to enter a well-structured dating scene replete with community-based *shadchanim*, singles weekends, and other organized activities aimed at helping single Torah-observant people meet each other under the proper circumstances.[2]

After the *chasunah*, after the first several years of marriage, after the first few children start to grow up and attend yeshivah, however, the *ba'al teshuvah* couple, now – to external eyes – settled community members, are often **still** dealing with unique lifestyle issues, issues that the *"frum* from birth*"* (FFB) may never have dreamed of.

Having conducted more that 120 parenting classes in communities around the world in the past several years, I have found it painfully obvious that there is a great and vital need to provide meaningful assistance to these wonderful, spiritual couples. They need help in dealing with their own unique specific issues, as their families grow and mature. Invariably, during the question-and-answer segment of the workshops, or privately, after the lectures, unique, *ba'al teshuvah* lifestyle-related questions come up. And they are difficult ones to answer:

It is a fortunate development when a *ba'al teshuvah* couple is able to relate happily and harmoniously with their non-Torah-ob-

---

2. This article is of necessity focusing on the majority of *ba'alei teshuvah* who are B'H able to find their mate. It is a sad reality that many *ba'alei teshuvah* – as well as many FFB singles – are not able to easily find their *zivug* and start a life together. We must continue to support the efforts of Invei Hagefen and other such organizations who are assisting these singles.

servant relatives. Obviously, this is not always the case. The *ba'al teshuvah* may be the only Torah-true Jew in his entire extended family. There is often very little support from family members. Sometimes there is open hostility or antipathy on the part of their non-Torah-observant relatives, or at best a resigned acceptance of the Torah-observant couples' particular brand of "fundamentalism."

Although elements from the past are often left behind when making the transition from a non-Torah-observant to a Torah-observant-lifestyle, there are some aspects of their previous lifestyle and relationships that cannot or perhaps should not be forgotten. These range from the strategic to the mundane, across a spectrum that includes how to relate to their parents (who are, after all, their FFB children's grandparents) and how to deal with the visiting family members during the couple's *simchos*. Even trickier is dealing with the extended family members as the *ba'al teshuvah* couple's children grow into adolescence. *Simchos:* to go, or not to go? What if my sister marries a gentile? What to do on Thanksgiving Day? Or Grandpa's 70th birthday party? "All the other grandchildren spend midwinter or summer break at Grandma's home in Florida. Why can't we go?" The list goes on and on.

The *ba'al teshuvah* family also has a stress shock when dealing with Torah-observant schools for the first time. Growing up in America, the *ba'al teshuvah*, particularly if he or she came from an affluent suburban area, perhaps went through an outstanding public school system. Funded with tax dollars, the American public school offered the pre-*ba'al teshuvah* an education replete with free music and art programs, low teacher-student ratios, extensive remedial programs, and a tremendous array of electives. Contrast that experience with the typical yeshivah, which, struggling with lack of funds, can offer little in these extracurricular areas.

Ba'al teshuvah parents living in communities blessed with a large Jewish population often have a number of yeshivos to choose from, presenting a variety of options. However, the parents in this situation are often unfamiliar with the distinctive attributes of the different yeshivos[3], and the nature of the admission process to mesivtos for their 8th grade *bachurim*.

Furthermore, as their sons (and daughters) mature beyond 4th and 5th grade, many *ba'alei teshuvah* find themselves intimidated by the prospect of learning with their children. This is a significant issue that must be dealt with.

Shabbosos and festivals can be a source of stress to the *ba'al teshuvah* couple as they struggle to learn the laws, customs, and nuances of these special times of the year. Many newly married *ba'al teshuvah* couples often feel rather lonely as their FFB friends are packing up to spend *Yamim Tovim* with their parents; after the third child, invitations to *sedarim* at FFB friends' homes seem to dry up.

Now that the children of the first generation of *ba'alei teshuvah* are reaching adolescence and *shidduch* age, they are dealing with new issues that require a great deal of guidance. While FFB couples deal with the same set of challenges, they often have a support group consisting of extended family members. They also have their own life's experiences to help guide them. To the FFB, the Torah and halachic dimension regarding adolescent issues and the marriage of a child is frightening enough. But the *ba'al teshuvah* often has little guidance. There are no books on this issue, no tapes to listen to, and no forums or formal support groups.

Our community has invested many millions of dollars and tremendous resources of energy in bringing *ba'alei teshuvah* to Yid-

---

3. For example, I am vigorously opposed to having *ba'alei teshuvah* parents send their sons and daughters to Yiddish-speaking yeshivos, if they do not speak Yiddish themselves. In my opinion, this virtually guarantees that the fathers and mothers will never be able to learn with their children. I am well aware that many of my colleagues would disagree with me, just as vigorously.

dishkeit. But the process cannot stop with the formal *ba'al teshuvah* institutions. The process of becoming a "successful" *ba'al teshuvah* is not a one-, two- or five-year process. It is probably not even a 25-year process. It is a life cycle process, and it might very well take two generations to be truly successful. We need to follow several guidelines to ensure that success:

1) We need to create awareness within our community that we must help acclimate these *ba'al teshuvah* families. Just because a *ba'al teshuvah* family has four or five kids and "seems to be doing all right" does not mean that it has mastered all the nuances and challenges of becoming integrated into the Torah world.

2) While numerous publications deal with becoming Torah-observant, the newly Torah-observant, and dating and marriage issues, there is a woeful lack of lectures, tapes, workshops, articles and books dealing with life cycle issues for the *ba'al teshuvah*.[4] Our community and Rabbinic leaders should recognize the opportunity to bridge the gap and fill the void with a rich selection of educational options for the *ba'al teshuvah* couple.

3) We should identify specialists within the *ba'al teshuvah* movement who can become "senior *ba'al teshuvah* advisers." These leaders would have specific training in providing advice to *ba'alei teshuvah* on many of the above-mentioned topics. These specialists would be available for consultation with *Rabbanim* as necessary. A growing

---

4. As a result of the feedback generated by this column, I organized a one-day "Life After Teshuva" Conference in Passaic N.J., addressing many of the themes raised in this essay. The presenters included Rabbi Shmuel Kaminetsky s'hlita, and renown experts in fields of kiruv and the acclimation of ba'alei teshuva families; Rabbis Avrohom Braun, Shlomo Goldberg, Yaacov Haber, and Yisroel Rokowsky. Tapes of the sessions can be purchased by emailing admin@rabbihorowitz.com or by calling 845-352-7100 x 133.

cadre of trained professionals in the *ba'al teshuvah* life-cycle field is needed to bring sufficient support for the *ba'al teshuvah* couple, ensuring that they have adequate resources to call upon in time of need or concern.

The *Ribbono Shel Olam* has given our generation a great gift – the thousands of sincere, committed, *ba'alei teshuvah* and their children. We must do all that we can to assist our brothers and sisters – *lach'sos tachas kanfei haShechinah*.

Chapter Twenty-Seven

KEEP YOUR CHIN UP

AN OPEN LETTER TO TEENS WHO HAVE LOST A PARENT

*D*ear reader:

Allow me to commend you for having the courage to read this letter. It is difficult enough to deal with all the ramifications of your loss each day without confronting the issue head-on in a more direct manner, which reading these lines will force you to do.

I strongly feel, however, that in the long term you will be better off for having done so. At this point in your lives, I really think that you should take advantage of the opportunity to draw strength from those who have experienced the same loss — and from an evolving understanding of the grieving process.

The notion of grief counseling didn't exist when my father died before my fourth birthday. My mother and her children — my sister, brother, and I — had to cope in the best way we could. Today, thankfully, things are very different. The horrible, searing pain of losing a parent doesn't get any easier. But in today's environment, professionals can help you explore your feelings and deal with your loss in a way that will help you cope and grow into adulthood with less difficulty. Additionally, a support group (such as Links) can help you draw strength from each other, fulfilling the timeless words of Shlomo Hamelech in *Koheles* (4:9), טוֹבִים הַשְּׁנַיִם מִן הָאֶחָד ... כִּי אִם יִפֹּלוּ הָאֶחָד יָקִים אֶת חֲבֵרוֹ — [The shared power of] two are better than one ... for if they should fall, one can lift the other.

My dear reader, I'd love to be able to tell you that the pain will go away one day, but I will never mislead you. I am so very sorry to say that the agony of losing a parent will never, ever really leave you. But it does get better slowly, over time. Growing into adulthood will perhaps enable you to cope better. Starting your own family will help you get back on your feet. Naming a child after your parent may soothe some of the hurt. But this tragedy is part of your life and you will need to deal with it on some level forever.

In my speeches and writings, I have always maintained that children who lost a parent are not in any "high-risk" category. True, we have challenges to overcome and mountains to climb that most others, thankfully, do not. But mountain climbing makes you stronger. Fired in the crucible of the pain and loneliness of losing a parent, most of us outgrow the inevitable "Why me?" phase, mature earlier than our peers, and become more sensitive human beings — having learned at an early age to appreciate life to its fullest. We, who remain behind in *shul* to face our sorrow alone while our carefree friends go out to enjoy each other's company during *Yizkor,* often develop a closer relationship with *Hashem,* as well, as time passes.

I once heard a touching story about the chassidic *rebbe,* Reb Levi Yitzchok, *z'tl,* who was referred to as the Berditchiver Rav. He once heard a crowd of people berating a man who was addressing *Hashem* in a loud and disrespectful tone after his cow had died. That animal was the sole source of income for this individual and his family, and he reacted to his pain by verbally lashing out at the *Ribbono Shel Olam* for causing him this loss. The Rav, who always looked for the good in people, raised his hands to heaven and exclaimed that he was envious of this man for the close and intimate relationship that he had with *Hashem.*

I guess that in a strange and similar way, those of us who were forced to confront our feelings with *Hashem* in our formative years, those of us who had to sort out the hurt, pain, confusion, and yes, at times, even anger, at having lost a loved one, hopefully come to a closer and more intimate relationship with Him, as well, over the course of time.

Keep your chin up, stay strong, and may Hashem continue to grant you *chizuk* and success.

(Rabbi) Yakov Horowitz

This letter appeared in Links, a magazine geared specifically to frum, teenaged girls who've lost a parent, and distributed free of charge to those in the situation and to educators. Links is a project of EITZAH, a Brooklyn-based chinuch organization. They can be reached at Links c/o Kohn 4219 12th Ave 2C Brooklyn, NY 11219 or olamhabo@verizon.net.

Chapter Twenty-Eight

YAHRTZEIT

hese questions are a compilation of some of the many that I have been asked over the years by children who have lost parents and/or the surviving parent/stepparent of the children.

DEAR RABBI HOROWITZ:

*ow do I properly observe a *yahrtzeit*? What does the word *yahrtzeit* mean anyway? Are there special things to say or do? Is it O.K. to be sad or moody on this day or should I just "deal with it" as some people seem to be telling me? How should I respond when the adults in my *shul* greet me on the day of the *yahrtzeit*? I keep hearing the words, "The *neshamah* should have an *aliyah*," from adults. What does it mean, and what should I do when people tell that to me? How can I get my friends to understand how difficult this day is for me, and how should I respond when they inadvertently make inconsiderate comments to me on this painful day?

RABBI HOROWITZ RESPONDS

The term yahrtzeit is a Yiddish term that is literally translated as "a year's time" (*yahr* means year, and *tzeit* is time). The term represents the anniversary of someone's death and is commemorated by the children, siblings, spouse, and sometimes parents of the deceased. The date of the yahrtzeit is calculated according to the Hebrew calendar. The most common practices observed on a *yahrzeit* are reciting *Kaddish*, lighting a special memorial candle that burns for 24 hours on the evening before the yahrtzeit, learning *mishnayos,* and visiting the graves of the deceased.

Jewish tradition and *hashkafah* teach us that humans are a unique hybrid of a physical body and a spiritual *neshamah.* When death occurs, one's *neshamah* takes leave of its body and ascends to the Heavens. At that time, the individual is judged for his/her actions and accomplishments spanning his/her lifetime. From that time onward, that *neshamah* cannot improve its standing in the Heavenly realm. However, according to *Chazal,* the *neshamah* receives a "review" of its original judgment on its yahrtzeit — with the opportunity to elevate its status in Gan Eden. How could things change after one passes on, you may think? In reality, the books are rarely ever closed on one's life since the *neshamah* almost invariably left behind a legacy during the time it spent in this world. Therefore, the secondary mitzvos it helped generate with its actions in this world still accrue after death to bring merit to the *neshamah.* For example, if one loans *siddurim* (prayer books) to a *shul* during one's lifetime, one gains a mitzvah each time someone uses that *siddur.*

The same concept would apply to one who helps start a *shul*, Jewish day school, or other *chesed* organization.

This concept most certainly applies to one who had children who lead meaningful lives, since they can bring merit to the *neshamah* of the deceased for many years to come.

This is where *you* come in, since children are the quintessential extensions of one's years on this world. Therefore, many of the *yahrtzeit* practices revolve around children generating mitzvos that accrue to the merit of their departed parent. We learn *mishnayos* or other Torah studies in memory of the departed *neshamah*. For many years, I would dedicate an extra hour's block of time all year long to learn a particular *Gemara* with the goal of completing it and making a *siyum* on my father's *yahrtzeit*. We say *Kaddish*, which prompts people to praise *Hashem* in response to our words. We take food and drink to *shul* so that people will make blessings on and enjoy the refreshments that were brought.

With all this in mind, the phrase that you hear many people greet you with on the day of the *yahrtzeit*, "The *neshamah* should have an *aliyah*," may become more meaningful to you. What they are telling you, especially those who knew your parent well, is that they, too, (obviously in a lesser sense than you) feel the loss of your parent and miss him or her. They are also expressing their sincere wish and hope that your departed parent will become elevated (*aliyah* — means go up, as in getting an *aliyah* in *shul* or making *aliyah* when one moves to Eretz Yisrael) in Gan Eden on this day. It is an expression of affection for your parent and for you, and a proper response would be to nod and say, "Thank you." Perhaps if you are up to it, consider expressing to them that you really appreciate their good wishes.

I think that it is perfectly O.K. to feel sad, moody, confused — or anything else — on the day of your parent's *yahrtzeit*. Just as different people celebrate victories and successes in a variety of ways, so, too, do people mourn losses in diverse fashions. The *yahrtzeit* day is a very difficult one, especially for those of us who lost parents at a young age. It is made more complicated by the fact that it is a normal day for everyone around us. Our friends at school — and later in life at work — do not understand that this day jars all sorts of unpleasant memories for us and it often feels as if a scab has been torn off a wound that has partially healed. So I would suggest to you that if you just feel as if you need some space to sort things out in your mind on the *yahrtzeit* day, then it may be a good idea to take part of the day off and do just that. Try not to be critical of people who say silly or inconsiderate things to you. Many of them feel rather awkward, because they don't really know what to say to you. Therefore, they may blurt things out that they did not intend to.

I would love to tell you that the *yahrtzeit* day gets easier with the passage of time, but at least in my case, and those of my close friends who lost parents at a young age, it really doesn't. I am writing these lines on the 44th *yahrtzeit* of my father, who passed away before my fourth birthday. And while the passage of time is a great healer for the other days of the year, I have found that in many ways the actual *yahrtzeit* day gets harder as time goes on. Every year, on the evening of my father's *yahrtzeit*, I tell my wife that I feel emotionally bruised and battered — as if a truck ran over me, *chas v'shalom*.

One thing that I always tell teens and young adults who have lost parents is to reach out for help if they feel bogged down by emotional overload. How bad does it have to be before you reach out for help? I would say that you should certainly go for help if you feel that the trauma of your parent's death is impeding your progress in school or in life. I would recommend that you consider going for grief counseling, contacting Chai Lifeline (www.chailifeline.org, 212-465-1300), a rabbi/*rebbitzen* in your community, or simply a grown adult who lost a parent at a young age. Mental health professionals have made such progress in the past few decades in understanding the grieving process and in helping family members sort out their emotions. Not taking advantage of this knowledge that is readily available is almost like getting a root canal without Novocain, or like a nearsighted person not using eyeglasses.

In the broadest sense, the best thing that you can do to honor the memory of your parent on the day of his/her *yahrtzeit* — and throughout the year — is to live a meaningful life. Having experienced wrenching pain at a young age equips you better than most others to be extraordinarily sensitive to others. You have sadly learned the value of time, the gift of life, and the opportunity that each day presents.

I give you my heartfelt *berachah* that you use these life-lessons to live a life of Torah and *chesed*, a life where you give and rarely take, a life where you heal and rarely hurt, a life where you leave the world a better place as a result of your words and deeds.

Living this type of life will bring eternal merit and *kavod* to your parent — and eventually to your own children.

Chapter Twenty-Nine

THE PIERCED TEEN AND I

I hardly ever sleep on airplanes. So after an 11-hour Thursday night flight to Eretz Yisrael, I arrived Friday noontime, jet lagged and exhausted. I came to spend Shabbos with our daughter, who was studying in a seminary in Yerushalayim. Together we walked through the winding streets of the Jewish Quarter and enjoyed a beautiful, spiritual *Kabbalas Shabbos* at the *Kosel*. After the conclusion of the *tefillos,* we returned to our hotel, which was almost exclusively occupied by Shabbos-observant guests, for the evening *seudah* (meal). I ate rather quickly and was in my hotel room getting some much-needed sleep by 7 o'clock. By midnight, I awoke, already having had a full night's sleep. I quietly left the room and made my way down to the lobby with a *sefer,* some reading material, and an assortment of roasted nuts that my daughter had purchased for me.

As I was sitting in the deserted hotel lobby, I looked up and noticed a teenaged young man sauntering through the lobby. He was wearing jeans and a T-shirt, sporting a spiked, Israeli version of a mushroom haircut and several body-piercing ornaments. Not your average *yeshivah bachur*.

I smiled in his direction, wished him *Shabbat Shalom*, and turned the bags of nuts in his direction as if to invite him to partake of them. He was a bit taken aback at my offer and asked me if I was sincere. When I assured him that I was, he sat down and eagerly made a significant dent in my supplies. Several minutes later, a few of his friends entered the lobby and he invited them over to join us.

Some picture that was — four secular teens and a chassidic, 40-something rabbi chatting in a hotel lobby over a growing pile of *garinim* shells. Once they found out that I was a school principal, we engaged in a lively discussion about their school life and I fielded seemingly endless questions about the yeshivah where I serve as *menahel*.

It was fascinating for me to observe how they warmed up to me as time passed. In fact, one by one they began referring to me respectfully, in the third person. Then, suddenly it got quiet for a moment or two. The young man who was the first to sit down wanted to know if he could ask me a question. "*Betach* — sure," I responded.

TWO IN A ROW

His eyes locked in on mine with a mixture of hostility and genuine curiosity. "Why are there no *charedim* like you (who are friendly and accepting) in Israel?" he asked me. I responded that there are thousands like me, but that he had simply never met any of them. I asked him if he ever had a Shabbat meal in a *charedi* home and encouraged him to try that experience — with an open mind. I even offered to set him up with one of many families who would be glad to have him over.

Then his friends joined in. "But why do they (*charedim*) hate us and throw stones at us?" they wanted to know. I told them that they should not believe the stereotypes about *charedim* that they have been reading in the papers. I informed them that only a tiny, vocal percentage of our community engages in this type of behavior. I politely but firmly pressed my point. I said that I have had insults and abuse showered on me over the years by individual secular Israelis as I walked the streets of Yerushalayim dressed in my *shtreimel*, but that I never assumed that any of the four of them were of that mind-set.

Like boxers circling each other in the ring, we weaved and bobbed around the issues they raised for a few more minutes until we parted company courteously and respectfully. I was so deeply disturbed by the conversation that I found it hard to concentrate on my *sefer* after the kids left the hotel lobby. I got up to stretch my legs and walked around the lobby for a few moments. If round one wasn't unpleasant enough, I got my second dose a few moments later. As I was walking to the rear part of the lobby, there was a secular woman finishing up a phone call on one of the hotel's pay phones. I greeted her with a polite *"Shabbat Shalom."* Her response was visceral and harsh. "Aren't you angry that I am speaking on the phone during Shabbat?" she asked me angrily.

In my barely passable Ivrit, I responded that anger was certainly not an emotion that came to my mind when I saw her on the phone. Saddened or upset perhaps, but angry? Why would I be angry?

FAMILY BREAKDOWN

I thoroughly enjoy every part of my visits to Eretz Yisrael. The *kedushah* (holiness), the predawn walks to the *Kosel* for *vasikin minyan* (sunrise prayer services), and perhaps most of all, watching our adult children progressively grow attached to the holy stones of *Artzeinu Hakedoshah*. But increasingly so, each of my trips to Eretz Yisrael leaves me feeling more and more troubled by the growing harshness and hostility between the secular and religious Jews. It's almost as if we are a behaving like a terribly dysfunctional family.

There is certainly more than enough blame to be placed on the leadership (and many individuals) of the secular community. I scan two secular Israeli papers every day, and the outrageous, inflammatory, anti-*charedi* comments are simply horrifying, and are so far beyond the pale of civilized discourse. I assume that the left wing, secular leadership of Shinui and Meretz will not be reading these lines. But if they would, I would tell them to search their souls and realize that they are depriving their children of the spiritual oxygen needed to sustain Jewish continuity by denigrating us so badly and repeatedly.

Having said that, don't we, too, need to undergo a *cheshbon hanefesh*? Whose insane idea was the rock-throwing anyway? Step back and think about it. Despite protests from *gedolim* against this practice, two generations of young *charedi* men **threw rocks** in a misguided effort to impress secular Jews with the *kedushah* of Shabbos and in an attempt to enforce its observance. Why in the world did we ever allow a fringe element to frame this debate, and why did we not forcefully and repeatedly distance ourselves from the violent actions of those who shamed us so? I am not discussing the somber and proper expressions of public and respectful protest at the pain of public *chillul Shabbos* sanctioned by our *gedolim*. We are discussing the lawlessness and desecration of *Hashem's* Name that took place in the guise of promoting Shabbos observance.

Chazal say that it takes 40 years to fully understand events that take place. Let's subject this issue of the rock-throwing *hafganos* (protests) that have taken place on and off over more than 50 years to the harsh light of cost-benefit analysis. What did it accomplish?

Close a few roads on Shabbos? Is that such a significant victory? Tens of thousands of *Yidden* have beautiful *Shabbosos* in America with cars driving all around them, albeit mostly driven by gentiles, which changes the dynamics of our response. However, I have a secular Jew living down the block in my hometown of Monsey. He drives and he washes his car on Shabbos. My wife and I greet him with a cordial *"Gut Shabbos"* when we pass his home. Each time, he responds with the same salutation — uttered with the utmost *derech eretz*. And even if the closing of streets in *charedi* neighborhoods was one in the win column, at what price was the victory?

OF RIOTING AND CUTS

A.M. Rosenthal wrote a nearly prophetic op-ed piece in the New York Times in 1992, following the disturbing Los Angeles race riots. He predicted that in the months and years following the riots, the upper-class whites in the country would riot in their own way. They would abandon the cities and move to the suburbs, he wrote, and they will vote Republican and shred the social services network. Sure enough, in 1994, two years later, Newt Gingrich was propelled to power and his "Contract with America" started a decade-long attack on funding for social programs. And shortly thereafter, President Bill Clinton announced that he would, "end welfare as we know it."

I conducted parenting classes in different Torah communities on three of the five evenings that I spent in Eretz Yisrael on this past trip. Fielding questions from hundreds of people in an open forum for two hours and taking private request for *eitzos* provided me with a very accurate understanding of the challenges that communities face. I can tell you firsthand that our valiant *avreichim* and their families are suffering terribly from the governments draconian "triple-whammy" social welfare cuts of the past few years.

Concurrently, child subsidies have been slashed, yeshivah funding has been cut back, and all sorts of regulations relating to religious schools are now in place — compounding the strain on these *mosdos haTorah.*

Shouldn't we ask ourselves if the recent, painful budget cuts brought about in part by the stunning ascendancy of Tommy Lapid and the Shinui party — the so-called "rioting" of the secular Jews — was even in a small part caused by the self-imposed collective black eye that we suffered as a result of the aggressive actions of some members of our community? We cannot avoid these implications for our future. Just because Tommy bungled his mandate and lost power does not mean that the forces that propelled him there have abated.

A HOPEFUL SIGN

I had the most wonderful five days in Eretz Yisrael, and thoroughly enjoyed the precious time that I spent with our daughter. But the events of Friday night cast a pall over my mood as I replayed them in my mind's eye again and again. Until Sunday morning.

It was about 7 o'clock in the morning — after the *vasikin* prayers in the *Kosel* Plaza. I was reciting *tehillim* after davening when I observed a scene unfolding right before me. Several secular Israeli teenagers had just arrived at the *Kosel.* They were dressed similarly to the young men that I had spoken to in the hotel lobby 36 hours earlier. Clutching paper yarmulkas on their heads, they kissed the holy stones of the wall and stood there in silence for a few moments. As they turned to leave, one teen in the group approached a bearded, elderly Sephardi Jew and asked him for a blessing. The boy bowed his head while the rabbi blessed him with feeling and vigor. His peers followed the lead of the first teen and received similar blessings. Those who were in close proximity to the rabbi watched this beautiful exchange with pride and *nachas*. But I suspect it was more meaningful to me than to the others — in light of my Friday-night experience.

The boys turned to leave and I went back to my *Tehillim*. I lifted my head again when the elderly rabbi loudly called the boys back to where he was sitting. He hugged the boys one at a time and warmly kissed each of them on both cheeks. He then placed his hands on their foreheads and emotionally exclaimed in Ivrit that *Hashem* should bless them and that all their actions should be met with unending success. They kissed his hand and walked away visibly touched. My eyes began to blur as I thanked *Hashem* for restoring my faith that future generations of His children will interact similarly with each other — with tolerance and true *ahavas Yisrael*.

Chapter Thirty

MY GRANDFATHER AND I

*M*y paternal great-grandfather was Rabbi Dov Ber Horowitz. Among *chassidim* throughout Europe, he was lovingly referred to as "Reb Berish Vishever," drawing on the name of the city in which he lived and faithfully served as *chazzan* and *shochet* for more than 50 years. Each year he wrote beautiful songs for *chassidishe Rebbeim* with whom he had close contact — among them the *Admorim* of Satmar and Vizhnitz, *zichronom livrachah*. Many of his *niggunim* (songs) are still sung today by *chassidim* around the world (among them, the Satmar *Sholem Aleichem niggun* and the Vizhnitzer *V'Emunah Kol Zos,* sung on *Shabbos Shirah* and *Shevi'i Shel Pesach*).

The great *tzaddik* and *gadol* Reb Shraga Feivel Mendelovitz *z'tl* used to ask my father *a'h* to sing his grandfather's stirring *Geshem/ Tal Niggun* every Shabbos during *Seudas Shlishis* in Torah Vodaas. To this day, Reb Shraga Feivel's 80- and 90-year-old *talmidim b'ezras Hashem* hum the tune to me when we meet at social gatherings. I honor my *zeide's* memory by singing his songs each Yom Tov meal, and my wife and I, with the *chesed* of Hashem, walked our children to the *chuppah* as dozens of my male cousins — Reb Berish's descendants — sang his beautiful *Geshem/Tal Niggun*.

In 1944 at the age of 72, Reb Berish and 3,000 of his townspeople, *h'yd,* were rounded up and deported to Auschwitz several days before Shavuos. On the loading dock waiting for the trains to arrive, surrounded by armed German troops and snarling dogs, Reb Berish rose and tearfully addressed the crowd of assembled Jews. It was late in the war and despite the fact that the people knew they were headed for almost certain death, escape was impossible under those conditions. Reb Berish encouraged his townspeople to turn inward and do *teshuvah* before they met their fate. Having served as *chazzan* in the town of "The Visheves" for 50 years, he knew all the *Yamim Nora'im tefillos* (High Holy Days' prayers) by heart. He used this knowledge and his beautiful voice to lead the entire assembled group in a word-for-word recitation of the closing *Ne'ilah tefillah* of Yom Kippur during their last few moments together.

Reb Berish was a victim of anti-Semitism — not only during his final years. Throughout his life government officials and civilians treated him and his contemporaries harshly. His opportunities for employment were limited, and he lived each day of his life in fear of pogroms and death.

Three generations have passed since those horrendous experiences. I, and to a much greater extent my children, have been raised, *Baruch Hashem*, in almost ideal circumstances in a *malchus shel chesed* (under the rule of a benevolent government). I can live where I wish to, engage in virtually any profession, and walk the streets of my neighborhood with a level of comfort and security almost unknown in *galus*.

Our immigrant parents never felt that level of security; and even those who did were sensitive to the fact that we are in *galus*. It is well known that Reb Yaakov Kaminetsky *z'tl*, during his years in Monsey, discouraged his *talmidim* from wearing *talleisim* (prayer shawls) in the street on Shabbos since he felt that we as Orthodox Jews should live modestly and not attract undue attention to ourselves.

My father never considered wearing a *tallis* in the street. People of my generation on the other hand, wear *talleisim* outside on Shabbos without giving it much thought. Our children don't even understand what the fuss is all about. Wear your *tallis*, or don't wear it; who cares?

I write these lines to share with you my growing sense of unease at the ill will that is being generated with our nonreligious and gentile neighbors over the many zoning and political battles that have emerged over the past years as a result of our exponential growth, *b'li ayin hara*, and our newfound political power. In some of the largest Jewish communities of North America, we are suddenly finding ourselves in the strange position of being a powerful force in the political arena. Elected officials in every level of government are courting us. In some cases, we even represent the deciding votes in our local races. Politics is often a nasty business, however. When these election campaigns kick into gear, otherwise reasonable people resort to negative attacks and smear campaigns against their opponents. In our eagerness to promote *our* candidates, we sometimes stoop to these tactics as well.

There are also significant issues of zoning and land-use matters across the United States that pit our real needs against the sensitivities, real or perceived, of our neighbors. Virtually every *shul* and yeshivah that is built is the focus of protracted, often bitter zoning battles. Having just completed a three-year odyssey to secure all approvals necessary to build the yeshivah where I serve as *menahel*,

I am intimately familiar with the passions that these situations generate on both sides.

As our community grows, *Baruch Hashem*, we will need *chochmas Shlomo* (the wisdom of King Solomon) to balance the need to pursue our rights while not violating *Hashem's* clear instructions to us — in the form of an oath — not to create ill will among our neighbors while we are in exile (*Kesubos* 111a).

With all these pots on the fire, we dare not provoke our neighbors needlessly over matters large or small that are within our power to avoid. In the past, this was self-evident as we were a small minority, and couldn't afford to engender any negative feelings. We also had a greater level of interaction with non-Jews in our neighborhoods than we do nowadays, which heightened our level of sensitivity to their feelings.

Things are very different now. In the last 60 years we have evolved from:

1. "Please allow us to live in peace," to
2. "I'm glad to be living in peace," to
3. "I have every right to live in peace," to
4. "We will always live in peace no matter what we do."

While I do not suggest that we march backwards to step 1, I think that a blend of steps 2 and 3 is the wisest path to take. This would follow the *shvil hazahav* (golden path) of moderation charted by the wisest of all men, Shlomo Hamelech (King Solomon). We should respectfully and vigorously advocate for our rights and privileges in this great country, but we must always be cognizant of the fact that our generation that lives in the United States has been granted the gift of security that eluded us for 2,000 years.

Rabbi Berel Wein, in one of his taped lectures, related that when his *shul* in Monsey was being built, and the main beam supporting the structure was being purchased, the contractor suggested that the *shul* invest in a more expensive beam, one with a 150-year guarantee. Rabbi Wein remarked that as a student of history, he is painfully aware that throughout our years in *galus*, Jews never planned to live in one place for that length of time.

If you accept my argument that step 1 is not an acceptable choice to live under and that a blend of steps 2 and 3 is the ideal, then please allow me to propose that the attitude of step 4 is downright dangerous. No one gave us a guarantee that this *menuchas hanefesh* (tranquility) will last forever. I was recently in Antwerp, where many observant Jews regularly remove their yarmulkas in the street for fear of being attacked. It is the same in many European countries. And if we ever needed a wake-up call as to how things can turn bad very quickly, just look at what has happened in France in recent years.

ACTING GRACIOUSLY — AND WISELY

*B*ut even if we choose to exercise our right to wear our *talleisim* in public on Shabbos, we should not walk four abreast across the street as our gentile or nonreligious neighbors are driving by. We should vigorously pursue our right to build *shuls* and yeshivos in our communities, but we should do whatever is humanly possible not to impede the flow of traffic and not to park illegally when attending those *shuls*. Our streets and lawns must be kept clean and tidy, and we need to be exceedingly polite to each other and to the nonreligious and gentile members that we interact with: on the roads, in the bank, in the post office, and at the supermarket.

We, as educators, parents, and community members, need to see to it that we do not follow the potentially disastrous path of step 4. We must pick and choose our issues and battles very carefully, and do our very best to conduct them with dignity and grace — even if and when we are provoked. We must do our very best to act as model citizens and be *mekadesh Shem Shamayim* (glorify the Name of Hashem) at all times. Our interactions with our neighbors must be in a manner of friendship and pleasantness, which is the way of our Torah.

Rabbi Naftoli Neuberger embodied this approach. He was a proud advocate for Torah values, and a prince among men, who conducted his affairs with outstanding distinction and refinement. In more than 50 years of exemplary public service in Baltimore, Maryland, he was revered among all segments of Baltimore Jewry and his opinion was sought by elected officials at local, state, and national levels — not for the votes that he delivered, but for his wisdom and unimpeachable integrity.

Each of us, as ambassadors for Torah Judaism, should seek to emulate his noble ways as we chart the course of our individual and collective lives in these difficult times.

Chapter Thirty-One

TIME FOR SOME QUESTIONS

In April 2006, an elderly Jewish man was arrested and roughly treated during a traffic stop in Brooklyn's Boro Park section. The arrest sparked a street riot — including teenagers torching garbage cans and a police car — covered by news outlets throughout the world.

Sadly the vast majority of those participating in the melee were Orthodox men and teens, many of whom were home for the pre-Pesach break.

My comments were written against the background of this distressing episode.

It is almost exactly one week after the *chillul Hashem* in Boro Park when fires were set in the streets and a police car was torched after a respected 75-year-old man was treated roughly by police officers while being issued a summons.

I spent this past Shabbos in Boro Park celebrating a *simchah* in our extended family. Walking the streets and enjoying the tranquility of Shabbos in a predominantly *Shomer Shabbos* neighborhood, it was hard to imagine that such mayhem had occurred in those streets just a few days previously. Over the course of Shabbos, I spoke to many people who were in the vicinity during the melee. The vast majority of adults spoke of their horror and disgust at what happened. Several people told me that they found it to be the most embarrassing experience of their lives.

If *charedi Yiddishkeit* were a product, I would suggest that we took a terrible body blow to our marketing campaign (which we refer to as our *kiruv* movement) as a result of the events of the past Tuesday. Don't believe me? Speak to anyone who works with or interacts with secular Jews or Gentiles and ask them how they enjoyed fielding questions about what happened in Boro Park last week.

Please note that I am separating the stimulus from the response. I do not wish to deal with the stimulus (the treatment of Mr. Schick by the police) – only our response to that stimulus. Discussing the facts of how Mr. Schick was treated distracts from the painful but necessary discussion about how our community responded to that stimulus – and what lessons we need to take from this devastating *chillul Hashem*. The fact is that some (and I stress, only some) of our children who were raised in our homes and attended our yeshivos acted like thugs and disgraced **ALL** of us.

There were clear and unequivocal quotes of condemnation of these illegal acts and calls for us to act as law-abiding citizens in this *malchus shel chesed* by both the Novominsker Rebbe, *shlita,* and Harav Rosenblum, *shlita,* in a full-page editorial in the *Hamodia* and many *rabbanim* condemned these lawless acts in their *Shabbos Hagadol* speeches.

Now, what? What do we, the people, need to do?

TIME FOR A CHESHBON HANEFESH

*I*ngrained in the hard drive of my mind are the teachings of my great rebbei'im who shared with us the notion that a *cheshbon hanefesh* (an enhanced level of reflection and introspection) is in order when something goes wrong in our lives and when we succumb to *aveiros* (sins). I think that a collective *cheshbon hanefesh* is in order after the recent events – one that will hopefully result in an improved set of circumstances in the future. For if we brush this off and do not explore the reasons and circumstances that created this embarrassing event, it will most certainly happen again. And let's be honest. This is not the first time these types of incidents have occurred, a fact noted by virtually all the newspapers when reporting this incident.

There are those who will undoubtedly fault me for airing our dirty laundry in public. To this I respond by pointing out that the charge of airing dirty laundry in public would be appropriate if I wrote an article about the private *shalom bayis* problems of a couple who came to me for guidance. However, this matter **already took place in public**. So it is already known. We *frum Yidden* are already taking far too many body blows in the public arena for these types of acts. I didn't *cause* this crisis melee or *chillul Hashem*. I am only responding to it. Every obviously *frum* person who interacts with non-Jews or secular Jews was bombarded with questions about this matter, and was shamed at having to defend the indefensible. As for the notion that I and the others who condemned these acts of hooliganism are adding to the criticism of the secular media, I say that our critics will most certainly find it refreshing and comforting that *frum* Jews are engaging in the type of appropriate and necessary reflection that will hopefully result in an end to this type of *chillul Hashem*.

HOW DID WE GET HERE?

So, I guess we collectively ought to take a long hard look in the mirror and ask ourselves:

How did this happen? What tinderbox was ignited that turned a group of fine spiritual, upstanding *bachurim* enjoying their *bein hazmanim* into two groups: 1) the tiny number who participated in these acts, and 2) the vast majority who stood by and did not interfere with the *chillul Hashem* that unfolded?

In the spirit of the Pesach Yom Tov, where asking questions is the order of the day, I pose some questions. I will not respond or editorialize (at least not now). I will only ask the questions, and allow you the reader to explore the answers. It is my hope that this will encourage you to discuss these questions with your spouse, friends, and children over the Yom Tov.

- Are we conveying to our children the incredible, unprecedented gift that they have, one that was denied our people for 2,000 years, the ability to live their lives in peace and tranquility. Do they appreciate it? Are we, for that matter, teaching enough Jewish history to our children?

- Are we repudiating these illegal actions unequivocally when they do occur with the same fervor reserved for other acts of *chillul Hashem* or for other sins against our Torah? Are we stating that they are morally wrong and against all teachings of our Torah?

- Where are our children learning these types of behavior? They certainly didn't see it in our homes. Is it from the secular media? Is it absorbed behavior learned from the protests of other groups seeking redress? (The Times and other papers reported that the kids were chanting, "No justice, no peace.") Is it a result of many *bachurim* returning from Eretz Yisrael where there is much more friction between the police and the *charedi* community? And, for each of these possibilities, what are we doing to ameliorate these influences?

- Do you believe that the secular media is biased against *charedi* Jews? And if so, do we just accept that fact, or should we do something about it? What can we do to improve our public relations?

- If the exact same mistreatment of a respected, elderly Jewish individual occurred in the Jewish communities of Scranton, Pennsylvania, or Seattle, Washington, would this type of protest occur? And, if you feel that it would not occur, why do you think it wouldn't?

- It is unquestionably the case that our neighborhoods and schools have become more insular over the past 30 years. That being the case, what are we doing to promote tolerance among our children, among different streams of *charedi* Jew, non-*charedi* Jews, non-religious Jews, and Gentiles – especially since there is often little meaningful interaction between them in predominantly *charedi* neighborhoods?

- How do our *charedi* children view the police? Devoted public servants who protect us? Devoted public servants who protect us and sometimes give out tickets? Irritating people who give out tickets? Irritating people who give out tickets in much greater proportion in *charedi* neighborhoods?

And, if I can paraphrase what our children ask in Yiddish after they chant the four questions: "Now that I asked the questions; will you, dear reader, please provide some answers?"

Chapter Thirty-Two

FINDING OUR VOICES — AND OUR NAMES

*W*hen the at-risk-teen issue was brought to the public consciousness, several Orthodox elected officials in the New York area pooled their resources to underwrite the production and dissemination of an excellent series of four videos titled "Shattered Lives" in order to raise public consciousness about the challenges that our teens-at-risk are facing.

In addition to parents, educators, and those who work with the at-risk-teen population, a number of Orthodox teens-at-risk were interviewed for the video series. The producers of this tape series afforded the kids complete anonymity by using a sophisticated computer program to garble the voices and distort the images of the young men and women who volunteered to be interviewed.

While these nameless, faceless discussions are entirely reasonable in the context of that particular video series, it is terribly disconcerting that much of the dialogue in Jewish communal life seems to be taking place under similar circumstances. Many or most people who write letters to the editors of *charedi* periodicals expressing their thoughts on these critical matters are not comfortable identifying themselves and the cities in which they live.

This reluctance is entirely understandable and proper when people are writing letters to the editor about delicate personal matters such as learning disabilities or personality disorders that they or their children may have. Otherwise, the reluctance to express *opinions* is quite troubling. We should all be comfortable expressing our views and thoughts in a rational and reasonable manner — agreeing to disagree respectfully, while defending our positions.

Sometimes, it borders on the comical. In my hometown of Monsey, New York, there are several weekly newspapers that are mailed to the community free of charge. I never cease to be amazed when people decline to sign their names in letters to the editor about mundane matters. Here are the types of letters that appear week after week:

> *"I would like to thank Town of Ramapo officials for doing such a wonderful job plowing the streets after last week's snowstorm."*
> — **E.R.**

> *"I really enjoy the Dvar Torah column every week."*
> — **Name Withheld.**

Whenever I read one of those letters, my first reaction is, "Wow, that was bold — you are really going out on a limb there!"

Speaking of comical scenarios, here is another. When people approach me and comment that they are pleased that I am writing columns that express sentiments they have been feeling for a long time, I sometimes (usually when my wife is not present) ask them, with a deadpan expression, if I can use their names in my next column, stating that they are supportive of my opinions. It is difficult to describe the horror in their eyes and the "deer-in-the-head-lights" look I get whenever I do this. I always walk away from these conversations saddened and worried — especially if they involve people who occupy high-profile positions in our *kehillos*.

What is most troubling is that the only voices that are being silenced are the moderate ones. Those in our community with the most extreme views comfortably thunder their protestations, in very public forums with nary a concern, while those who have more mainstream views are often reluctant or afraid to express them.

We are paying a terrible price for this silence and for the suppression of communal dialogue. When important problems are not honestly discussed and addressed, they fester and grow. In the darkness of neglect, manageable challenges become full-blown emergencies. In a climate of fear, extremist "solutions" to real problems often set the stage for much larger calamities later on.

We all know the incredible successes of our *chareidi kehillah*. We are raising, with the *chessed* of *Hashem*, thousands of proud, idealistic young men and women, devoted to our timeless *mesorah*. Our yeshivos and *kollelim* are filled with vigor and positive energy. We have more than earned our right to celebrate these accomplishments. But there are incredible challenges ahead.

Like it or not, ready or not, we — and our children — are being thrust into a rapidly changing world where all the rules are changing. Instant and exponentially growing methods of communication have already broken the protective "fire wall" we so carefully built around our homes and communities. And this process will only accelerate as time marches on.

We desperately need forums where communal matters are candidly discussed in an environment of mutual respect, with an eye toward generating solutions to these challenges. We need to provide forums where moderate views are encouraged and appreciated and where those who care enough — and have the courage — to ask tough questions are respected for their dedication to the future of our children.

Chapter Thirty-Three

YOUR CHILD'S TEEN YEARS

everal years ago, after a parenting talk that I gave on the subject of at-risk teens, there was an extended question-and-answer segment. During that time, a man got up and asked with great emotion, "O.K., Rabbi; now what?" There was pin-drop silence in the room and many heads nodding in complete agreement as I contemplated my response to his question.

NOW WHAT?

ruth be told, the feelings that this gentleman expressed are the sentiments shared by many parents these days. "O.K., you now have our attention. We agree that there are real issues that need to be addressed. We are frightened and perhaps confused. Now, what are we supposed to do about it?"

I turned on the microphone and softly responded, "Now, we need to parent."

The honest answer is that the skill-set that our parents used when raising us – or for that matter, what we may have used when raising our children when they were younger – may just not be enough anymore.

HANDS-ON AND EFFECTIVE PARENTING — YOUR CHILD'S BEST HOPE FOR SUCCESS

No, not all problem children are the result of bad parenting. There are so many educational, social, and emotional factors that have a significant effect on your child's success in school and in life, many of them beyond your control. However, without a doubt, effective parenting can be helpful in dealing with a difficult (or an easy-to-raise) teenager.

The ubiquitous and highly effective "Parenting – The Anti-Drug" ads that have been running for the past few years were a direct result of the voluminous research conducted over the past two decades. The studies indicated that the greatest pre-determining factor in the success of children – and their ability to stay trouble - and drug-free throughout adolescence — was the involvement of effective and knowledgeable parents in their lives.

The objective of these columns on adolescents is to help you with your *first* teenager. By the time you have raised your second or third teenager, you'll be able to write columns of your own, if you can find the time and energy. I hope that this series of articles will help speed up the learning process, and help you raise your oldest teen effectively and painlessly.

Chapter Thirty-Four

TEEN TRANSITION

The first step in effectively raising your teenage children is to recognize that their behavior is not a personal attack. It's not about you. It's about them. *It's always about them.* Remembering that may help you parent more effectively.

Physiologically, their hormones are raging; spiritually and psychologically, they are in transition between childhood and adult life with all its responsibilities. Their future is unknown: Who are they? Who will they be? How will their relationship with Hashem evolve and develop? Marriage, children, and careers loom on the horizon. Despite their tough pose, our teenagers are often very insecure and frightened. It is this insecurity that fuels so many of the behaviors that we find so difficult to deal with.

AN INTERESTING OBSERVATION

*I*t is interesting to note that the Torah, in its eternal wisdom, made allowances for adolescent behavior. Boys before the age of thirteen (twelve for girls) are exempt from mitzvah obligations, except that parents must train them according to their growing levels of maturity. After age 13, a young man or woman is treated as a fully grown adult in Beis Din (religious court), but they are not accountable in the Heavenly Court until age 20.

During teenage years, from age 13 to age 20, they are obligated to make restitution for all damages incurred and are liable to make good on all their commitments. However, during this phase, they are not punished for any spiritual transgressions that do not affect other people (*bein adam l'makom*).

The message seems to be pretty clear. We need to hold teens responsible for damages, lest they wreak unbridled havoc. But, at the same time, Hashem affords them a level of understanding for their adjustment period — or "temporary insanity."

And despite the passage of thousands of years, the bookends of this phase have not changed (13-20; exactly the teenage years).

PUSHING OFF

*T*eenagers often model the independence stage of toddlers – "The Terrible Two's" — breaking away and then running back to make sure we're still there; trying new experiences on their own and coming home to "refuel."

What complicates matters is that teenagers often find it difficult to acknowledge their need for our support, love and guidance. It is so critically important for parents to ignore the sometimes irritating behavior of their adolescent children and realize that they need to provide that stability and unconditional love when their teenage children are in need of it.

UNDERSTANDING YOUR ROLE IN ALL THIS

*I*n your desire for closeness, don't confuse your role. You are not their friend. You must guide them whether they claim to like it or not. Teenagers need rules and structure and they need to be able to look to you for direction.

A leading *rosh yeshivah* shared a beautiful metaphor with me several years ago. He said that he often feels like Yaakov Avinu (see *Bereshis* 32:24, note the comments of Rashi and others) who stood in middle of a stream and transported his children and possessions from one side of the river to the other.

It's as if our teenagers are standing on one side of a raging river filled with rapids and strong currents. Our job is to help them navigate these treacherous waters and end up safely on the other side. (I always found it interesting that Yaakov Avinu was placed in this role at a time when many of his sons were in their adolescent years.)

NO ONE EVER SAID IT WOULD BE EASY

*I*t is a scary, dangerous, and new territory for both parties. But it is your mission and sacred responsibility to help them with this transitional phase in their lives. No one else can do it for you — or as well as you can.

Their peers are extremely important to them, like a second family. And if teenagers forced to choose between the acceptance of their peers and the love of their parents, don't be surprised if they pick the former. But don't for a moment believe that your input doesn't matter. Always remember that if you parent effectively, you still will be, by far, the most powerful force in their lives. You will frame their value system and give them the moral compass that will guide them through life's travels.

Chapter Thirty-Five

LETTER FROM YOUR TEENAGE CHILD

Dear Mommy and Daddy:

Imagine how you would feel if you were told that in two years from today, our entire family would need to relocate to a different part of the country. You would certainly be quite concerned – for good reason. Think of all the questions you would have. Here are just a few of them:

Where will we live?

Will we be able to find jobs in the new location?

Will we be prepared for those new positions?

Will we make new circles of friends?

How about our old friends – will we still stay close?

What will our standing be in our new community?

Now, imagine what your anxiety level would be like if you would not be able to answer a single one of these questions.

WELCOME TO OUR WORLD

*W*elcome to our world.

Mommy, Daddy, I only posed these questions to you so that you would gain some understanding into my world.

You always say that you remember what it was like to be a teenager. I think that you may remember what it was like when you were my age — but this is me, not you.

Come to think of it, I only asked you a few of the questions that go through my mind. There are so many more.

Will I get into a good high school and seminary?

Which one?

Who will I marry?

Will I marry?

How am I supposed to figure out who to marry?

Will I have a great marriage or will we fight all the time like some of my friends' parents?

Will I have children?

What will they look like?

Will I be able to afford to give my kids the things that we have at home?

CHANGING

These past few months you both have been complaining about how I am changing. You say that you don't recognize me any more. We are arguing more than we ever did. **Well, I *am* changing!** My body is changing, my mind is changing, and my life is changing. We both have to deal with that. I am not 8 years old any more. I still love you very much, but I need to move on and get my own life. And the thing that frustrates me is that I can't seem to discuss things with you without a full-blown argument over my clothing, my friends, my language; whatever! I thought that writing things down in a letter might help you understand the big picture – what it is really like to be a teenager. I am hoping that you will come to understand why my friends are so important to me, why I "zone out" sometimes; why I get moody and impatient, and roll my eyes (sorry about that) when you lecture me. I hope you will read this carefully. It was quite difficult to write this letter, but I'm hoping that it will be a good first step in improving our relationship. Because I love you more than anyone in the world.

Love,
Adina

SENDING YOUR TEENAGE SON OR DAUGHTER TO ERETZ YISRAEL

PART ONE

*O*ver the past few decades it has become the norm for many or most of our sons and daughters to spend a year or two, post-high school, in Eretz Yisrael. For the vast majority of our youngsters it is a remarkable period in their lives, an uplifting, life-altering experience, as they grow spiritually and emotionally, gain a sense of independence, and they carry with them the memories of their moving experiences of studying in our Holy Land for the rest of their lives.

In light of the challenges posed by sending boys and girls in their late teens 6,000 miles from home, I think it is imperative for parents to become more educated about the enormous benefits of the year in Eretz Yisrael, and the significant challenges that your children will face during that time.

MY ROLE IN THIS PROCESS — AND YOURS

I think the most productive role that I can play would be to:

1) empower parents by framing the questions and issues that will enable you to make appropriate decisions for your children.

2) share with you some of the wisdom of experts in the field — *mechanchim*, educators, and mental health professionals.

3) cut through some of our collective denial by offering you some facts on the ground and sharing with you the perspective of our teenagers.

For the purposes of this discussion it is most helpful, I think, to consider the collective body of our teenagers as a continuum ranging from quiet, respectful, obedient children, who are well adjusted, and high achievers at school. At the other end of the spectrum would be youngsters who are unfortunately addicted to drugs and/or alcohol, defiant, and to date, unproductive in school. Obviously, most of our children fall somewhere in between these bookends.

I prepared an evaluation sheet for parents to use in the process of evaluating the risk level of their child. It may also be a good idea for your child to complete this form independently as a form of reflection and self-evaluation. Getting a reflective, honest read on your child can be a very helpful tool in evaluating his or her readiness to spend months and years away from home. In my next essay, I will discuss in detail many of the issues and attributes raised in the evaluation sheet — and their ramifications for your child. Please note that I purposely did not assign acceptable final scores or values for this sheet. I leave that for parents to do. But be aware that for each of these questions, a lower score means that your child is in a lower risk category. This only means that the risk is lower, not that there is no risk. Away from home, substance use, abuse, and dependence happen to high achievers, who, while under the care of their parents, did not have a history of drug use, according to Lewis Abrams, LCSW, CASAC, Executive Director of the Yatzkan Center. He advises parents to carefully check the level of supervision in the schools their children attend and to maintain contact with their kids — and a school person they have confidence in — throughout the "year." A higher score on this evaluation sheet means that your child is at greater risk of spiraling downward in Eretz Yisrael or in the States if not placed in a setting that provides solid education and appropriate supervision.

ASSESSING YOUR POST-HIGH SCHOOL CHILD (AND HIS OR HER READINESS FOR A YEAR IN ERETZ YISRAEL)

ACADEMIC SUCCESS

My child:
1. has done very well in school.

2. has done well in school.

3. is an average student.

4. is a poor student, whose grades are dropping.

5. has failed many subjects throughout school.

LEARNING PROFILE

My child can best be described as:

1. loves to learn — spends lots of after-school-hours learning

2. studious and conscientious.

3. has average studying habits.

4. is uninterested in school.

5. has significant learning disabilities.

CONNECTION TO JUDAISM

1. My child observes all mitzvos meticulously.

2. My child is fully observant.

3. My son would not daven with a *minyan* if there was no social pressure or if school was out.

4. My child would not daven at all if there was no supervision.

5. My child feels no connection, but we are hoping that "the year" will turn him around.

ATTITUDE TO AUTHORITY FIGURES IN PREVIOUS SCHOOLS

Over the past five-six years, my child:

1. got along well with all school faculty members — still maintains close contact with a former teacher.

2. got along well with most school faculty members.

3. got along well with the (few) school faculty members that he or she respected.

4. had constant run-ins with school faculty members.
5. never did well in school, was suspended many times, and switched schools.

THRILL SEEKING

My child:
1. is rather subdued.
2. tends to follow wild friends, but is not a leader.
3. is looking for "a buzz" (thrill), loves to party, and goes "clubbing."
4. is sadly out of control.

MATURITY

My child is:
1. mature beyond his or her years — deserves my complete trust.
2. average in maturity — I need to keep a careful eye.
3. a bit irresponsible — needs close supervision.
4. very irresponsible.

MOTIVATION

My child wants to go to Eretz Yisrael to:
1. grow spiritually.
2. be with his or her friends.
3. have a great time.
4. get away from home.

AGE

My child is:

1. 21 or older.
2. 19-21.
3. 17-19.
4. below the age of 17.

HOBBIES AND SPORTS

My child has:
1. many hobbies and loves to play sports, spends his or her spare time productively.
2. some hobbies — usually spends his or her spare time productively.
3. very few interests; we are worried about how he or she is spending free time.
4. basically has no recreational interests.

CIGARETTE SMOKING

My child:
1. never smoked.
2. has an occasional cigarette.
3. smokes socially — in a crowd.
4. smokes regularly, but claims that he or she is not addicted.
5. is a heavy smoker.

ALCOHOL

My child:
1. never drinks.
2. has an occasional drink — or two.
3. drinks quite a bit on *Shabbosos* and at weddings, but no other times (we hope).

4. drinks heavily on *Shabbosos* and at weddings, gets drunk from time to time.
5. is a heavy drinker, gets drunk repeatedly and intentionally.

Chapter Thirty-Seven

SENDING YOUR TEENAGE SON OR DAUGHTER TO ERETZ YISRAEL

PART TWO

In the last essay, I included a risk-assessment form designed to assist parents in evaluating their children. Now, I would like to spend some time discussing in greater detail some of the issues raised in the questionnaire.

ACADEMIC SUCCESS AND LEARNING PROFILE:

*Y*our child's past academic success is an extremely important issue to consider when contemplating sending a child to Eretz Yisrael for the year.

In assessing appropriate school settings, you may wish to consider:

Does your child have a track record of success in previous years in school?

How is his or her attitude to studies?

Are there any learning disabilities?

Have you had any testing done in the past?

Is it possible that there are learning disabilities that may have gone undiagnosed?

All of these factors should be considered in your decision-making process as you search to find the right program for your child. If your child has been learning well and is achieving success, it is, in theory, easier to find a program that is geared to his or her needs. If your child's learning profile requires specific attention, it may be more challenging for you to find a program geared to his or her needs.

GETTING IN, OR GETTING ON

*V*ery often, parents are (rightfully) anxious about the application and admission process and may be tempted to withhold information about learning issues regarding their child. Although this attitude may be entirely understandable, it is usually counterproductive. If you are worried that sharing this sensitive information may turn off potential schools, those schools are probably not right for your child. Bear in mind that getting your son or daughter into a school is not the most important objective. Getting into a school where your child *will thrive* is what you should be considering. Placing your son or daughter in a school setting for which they simply are not equipped — or that is not equipped for them — will often result in frustration and anxiety for your child and the faculty members. Parents should be aware of the trap of selecting a "prestigious" school because it will look good on the resume; the key is to select a school best suited to the child. If your child has a specific learning profile and requires an educational program to address these needs, you will be well served to share this information with prospective schools.

HOBBIES:

A huge question for parents to address, primarily as far as boys are concerned, is: What will our child do during his or her downtime? Please be aware that there is a great deal of unstructured time — in the evenings, on weekends, and especially during *bein hazemanim* breaks such as the summer months and around the *Yamim Tovim*. Your child will have blocks of time with little or no structured activity. In future essays we will be discussing preparing your children for independence, the prospective school's attitudes toward these times, and their level of supervision. But it is important to consider your child's profile as well. Unless your son is a true *masmid* (diligent student) who learns every free moment, he will have large slots of time on his hands.

I attended Yeshiva Torah Vodaas high school and *Beis Midrash* in the 1970's. We had the highest-caliber *limudei kodesh* program, and a rigorous program in general studies. We had the *zechus* of hearing *shiurim* from some of the great minds of prewar Europe. Nearly 25 percent of my classmates earned Regents Scholarship Awards. (The New York City general population was averaging 4-5 pecent

Regents Scholarships at that time.) We also played basketball and other sports for two or more hours every single day. Many of the leading 40-and-50-year-old *k'lei kodesh* and communal leaders of the current generation were outstanding *masmidim* ... and very good basketball players.

I think it of great value for children to have healthy hobbies in their formative years, and opportunities for exercise. I also attribute the exponential growth in cigarette smoking and alcohol consumption among our teens partially to the lack of opportunities for early-and-frequent exercise in school and on the weekends. Children, especially boys, who do not have hobbies, play sports, or find healthy recreational activity are more likely, in my opinion, to engage in smoking, drinking, "clubbing" or other dangerous activities. I therefore included a lack of hobbies as a risk factor. Which brings me to ...

VICES:

*S*orry to be so blunt, but cigarette smoking is much more prevalent among our teenage boys than we would care to believe, and alcohol consumption is far, far too high. Don't believe me? Don't trust the other "talking heads"? Then, do your own homework.

Here are some ideas:

Ask several teenage boys what percentage of their friends are smoking (I did, and the answers range from 20-50 percent, or more).

Ask your local Hatzolah member about calls he has responded to due to teens overdoing it with alcohol. There are even horror stories of teens who have become nearly comatose or beyond from alcohol overdoses due to hard, unsupervised drinking at vorts, weddings, and other parties.

Obviously, these are exceptions rather than rules. Most of our sons and daughters are doing well or wonderfully in school. But we need to address these issues and realize that we are not immune to their ramifications.

And please get to know your child before you consider sending him (or her) to Eretz Yisrael — where there is no legal drinking age, and cigarettes are available in vending machines.

Chapter Thirty-Eight

Proactively Addressing the *Chinuch* Challenges of Our Generation

*O*ver a decade ago, I began writing, "An Ounce of Prevention" — the article that dramatically changed the course of my life. It appeared in the May 1996 issue of *The Jewish Observer* and candidly addressed a topic that was simply not discussed in polite company at that time — the subject of our beloved boys and girls who were not making it in our yeshivah system.

The Jewish Observer got more than fifty letters to the editor — the most ever in response to a published article — and more than 300 people called my home phone in the first month alone. A small percentage of the letters and calls complimented or took issue with some of the things I had written. But the vast majority of them were from desperate parents looking for help — any kind of help — in getting their children back on the path to successful lives. Clearly, a sensitive nerve had been touched.

Following sessions on the topic of at-risk teens at the national conventions of Torah Umesorah and Agudath Israel, and with the active encouragement of our *Gedolei HaDor*, Project YES was created with a sacred mission — to help each and every one of our precious children achieve success in our *yeshivos* and Beis Yaakovs.

Since that time, many positive developments have occurred as a result of the attention devoted to this critical issue. Wonderful organizations and tailored educational programs have been created to help children who are not making it in mainstream schools. Parenting classes and in-service training for *rebbei'im/moros* have become accepted in our circles. There is a far greater degree of sensitivity to "children at-risk."

But I am deeply, deeply concerned about the potential for a huge, increase in the number and percentages of our children who may *r'l* abandon Yiddishkeit in the coming years if we do not transform the way we parent and educate our children. I have been feeling this way for a few years now, but this uneasy sentiment is growing as time goes on.

Why all the worry, you ask? Are we not doing extraordinarily well in the arena of raising our children? The answer is that we most certainly have so much to be proud of. *Batei midrashim, kollelim,* and seminaries are brimming with many thousand of outstanding, spiritual young men and women, *kein yirbu*. We have demonstrated our ability to transmit our timeless tradition to our children and grandchildren. But that is only part of the story — the enjoyable part. However, there are components of the bigger picture that are out of sight and therefore conveniently out of mind.

I'd like to ask you to conjure up a mental image of the dancing in the men's section of the last wedding that you attended. In your mind's eye, there are probably several concentric circles of participants — each of them with varied levels of intensity. In the inner circle, you have the *chosson* and his friends dancing with great fervor. The second ring probably consists of middle-aged guys (like myself) operating at a much slower RPM (for readers who occupy the inner ring at weddings, RPM stands for revolutions per minute), while the outer circle of the dance is comprised of SMV's (slow-moving vehicles). In addition to these three groups, you have individuals sitting at tables not partaking at all in the festivities. Finally, there are those outside the wedding hall, smoking or chatting on their cell phones.

Now imagine if you asked people from these diverse groups for their perception of the dancing at the wedding. The inner, lively group would say that the dancing was fantastic. Middle-aged guys would say the music was too loud for their taste. Outer group members may tell you that the boys were a bit on the wild side. And the fellows outside on their cell phones will say, "Dancing? What dancing?"

That is a thumbnail sketch of the children our community is raising. The "inner group" — those achieving success in our schools — is doing extraordinarily well, *Baruch Hashem*. The "middle group" thinks that some things are too intense for them, but they are still very much part of the community, while the "outer group" operates at the fringes of our society, participating only marginally and feeling rather disenfranchised. And then there are the people outside the wedding hall ... those who completely abandoned Yiddishkeit. So, how are we doing as a society in the raising of our children? Well, it depends on your vantage point.

If I may stay with the wedding analogy for another moment, I am that restless fellow who bounces around among the three dancing rings — and keeps running out to chat with the guys outside the hall. You see, there is an extraordinary dichotomy in my professional life (or rather, lives). Daytime, I am the quintessential inner-ring participant. I serve as the *menahel* of a yeshivah elementary school, where I get to walk the hallways and listen to the sweet sounds of *tefillah* (prayer) and the beautiful singsong chanting of the timeless Torah thoughts of Abaya and Rava (two sages of the Talmud). But as the sun sets each night, I am confronted with the horrific agony of the children who are not succeeding in our school system and the unspeakable anguish of their parents, siblings, and grandparents. The phones at Project YES and so many other outstanding organizations ring with stories of frustrated, unhappy children; with reports of gambling, drug abuse, and other horrible activities — even deaths and suicide.

What are the numbers? Accurate information and research-based studies are not readily available, but the reality is that far too many children from observant homes have completely left Yiddishkeit.

However, viewed from an historical perspective, the "drop-out" rate from Orthodox Jewry in the past fifty years is far lower now than it was during the tumultuous hundred years that preceded the generation of our parents — from 1850 to 1950. The "drop-out" rate was much, much higher in the Lower East Side at the turn of the century, in Yerushalayim in the Thirties and Forties, and in many Chassidish, Litvish, and Ashkenazic communities in pre-war Europe when communism, pogroms, and grinding poverty decimated the ranks of the frum community.

We are deluding ourselves — and ignoring the lessons of history — if we think that we are somehow immune from tidal wave of children leaving Yiddishkeit in the years to come. The frantic pace and intensity of the "inner ring" has grown over the past 10-15 years. And as the dancers are clasping their hands tighter and tighter, more of those in outer rings are finding it difficult to keep pace, and they are waiting and watching — not sure if they want to join the dance or just go outside for a smoke and a schmooz.

All the while, there are enormous external cultural changes occurring that have profound ramifications for the Torah-observant community. More than seven years ago, I delivered a lecture at a public forum regarding the challenges presented to Torah families by rapidly evolving technology. An individual on the panel who preceded me spoke about the need to "circle the wagons" — keep these influences away from our children. I followed his presentation by stating that I agreed wholeheartedly that parents must be very vigilant about what their children are exposed to, as I have repeatedly stated at virtually every parenting class that I conduct. But I also said that this will not nearly be sufficient, as I predicted that within ten years, our children will be able to go to the local candy store and purchase a disposable palm-size device for $25 (along the lines of a phone card) that will allow them to set up their own email account and go on-line without their parents ever knowing about it. I then spoke about the need to effectively parent our children and see to it that they are in nurturing school and community environments.

I keep getting calls from concerned parents from charedi and Chassidish homes asking me how to respond to their teenage children's requests for iPODs. These are sheltered children from "heimishe" homes. Their parents are rightfully terrified of what the implications are for saying *yes* to the request, but correctly realize that saying *no* to the request without a good reason will be counterproductive. They also fully understand that their children can buy it without their permission if they really want to.

What is also unsettling is the fact that many of these parents have no idea what an iPOD is. So there you have it. Kids speaking a language that their parents don't understand. Children acclimating to a new environment while their parents are like ... well, immigrants. The last time we had that experience was on the Lower East Side. Do you have any idea what percentage of the kids left Yiddishkeit in that generation?

People are always asking me how things are doing these days regarding the teen-at-risk crisis. In response to these questions, I usually nod my head and make small talk, as the settings in which these questions are presented are generally not conducive to serious discussions. And to be perfectly honest, I have found that most people don't really want to hear my perspective on the stark reality.

But if you wish to know my candid thoughts on this subject, pull up a chair and read what I have to say. It will probably upset you. You may disagree with my assessment. I may engender your resentment and perhaps even your anger for writing these pieces and airing these subjects in such a public forum. But I feel an overwhelming sense of responsibility to write these articles, nonetheless.

For we need to candidly discuss how we educate our children and how we set our charity priorities. We need to talk about investing in the training and financial stability of our valiant *mechanchim/ mechanchos,* and discuss the need to provide recreation opportunities for our kids. We need to reflect on the missions of our schools — are we looking to raise only *mitzuyanim/mitzuyanos* (outstanding students) or also average, well-adjusted children who have the capacity to become *mitzuyanim/mitzuyanos?* Should average or weaker students be relegated to second-tier schools, or should they be welcome in mainstream schools? We need to have candid discussions about how to confront the challenges of technology that are heading our way — ready or not. The list goes on and on.

I hope that these columns will help us realize our collective goal of *"V'chol bo'nayich limudei Hashem* — And all your children will be students of Hashem" (*Yeshaya* 54:13).

Chapter Thirty-Nine

SunBlock, Anyone?

Moving From Intervention to Prevention

*I*magine that you work in a pharmacy during the summer months. All day long, day after day, people hobble into your store suffering from the effects of painful sunburn injuries. Well, you are a compassionate person, so you dutifully guide them to the section of the drugstore where they can purchase the various sprays, creams, and lotions that treat sunburn pain. One would imagine that after a while you would be quite motivated to direct all customers to purchase a tube of sunblock and a hat. After all, for a tiny investment of time and money, one could prevent sunburn rather than treat it – and avoid many days of horrible anguish.

When Project Y.E.S. was created, I was given a sacred mission by our Torah leaders, members of the Moetzes Gedolei HaTorah, and the legendary president of Agudath Israel, Rabbi Moshe Sherer, z'tl, to help the children who were not succeeding in our glorious yeshivos and Bais Yaakov school system.

I am very proud of the lifesaving work that our Project Y.E.S. staff members and volunteers have done over the past 10 years. I am inspired by the outstanding work of the many organizations who have dedicated resources and energy to help our precious children succeed – in school and in life. I am touched by the overwhelming generosity of the donors who have responded magnificently to requests to fund these programs.

But even a cursory analysis of the teens-at-risk scene begs the question: "Why aren't we spending more time, effort, and resources on prevention rather than on intervention?" Surely there are reasonable steps that we can take to avoid at least some of the heartache of teens at risk, if we have the fortitude and courage to honestly evaluate how we parent and educate our children.

The first step in this process should be to spend some time reflecting on the factors that place our children at risk. Then, moving forward, analyze each of the risk factors and decide what can be done to address each one before they become full-blown problems. The challenge with that process is that we all approach this issue from the perspective of our life experiences and with our preconcluded biases.

I was once traveling in a subway train from Brooklyn to Midtown Manhattan with a close friend of mine who had lived in Eretz Yisrael all his life. He had just arrived in America for medical treatment the previous evening and was rather overwhelmed by the organized chaos of the rush-hour scene in the New York City subway system. After observing several successive stations filled with many hundreds of people trying to squeeze in our packed train, he asked me in all innocence, "Don't you have *k'vishim* (highways) in America?"

Well, if you think about it, the response of many or most people to the question, "What is the primary cause for the teens-at-risk crisis?" is rather similar to that of my friend in the subway train. For it is part of the human experience to view things from one's own perspective. A family counselor may tell you that poor parenting or lack of *shalom bayis* are the leading causes of teens abandoning *Yiddishkeit*. A stay-at-home mom will inform you that the explosion of day care caused by financial demands and working mothers are causing our children – and their issues – to be neglected. A mental health professional may claim that improper treatment is the leading cause, while the manager of a charity organization will point to grinding poverty as a terrible risk factor. A *kiruv* professional may inform you that some children just aren't finding fulfillment in our Torah lifestyle the way it is currently being presented to them.

As we can well imagine, the answer is much more complex. While each of the risk factors noted above is valid and needs to be addressed if we are to make a significant dent in the number of children dropping out of our Torah society, no single one of them can be listed as a primary reason all the time. It is inaccurate to assume that completely solving any one of the issues noted above would bring the teens-at-risk crisis to a screeching halt.

I, too, plead guilty to the syndrome noted above. For, although I wear many hats, I am primarily an educator, which invariably affects my view of things. With that in mind, it is entirely understandable that many of the columns in this series addressed educational aspects of the teens-at-risk issue. However, as the primary focus of this series of essays is to prevent what I see as the clear and present threat of an exponential increase in the number of our precious children abandoning *Yiddishkeit* in the years ahead, we would probably be better served to broaden the theme of these essays and to scan things through a wider lens.

As is the case with all matters of consequence, we will need the wisdom and guidance of our *gedolim* when considering how to adapt

to the changing landscape of parenting children in these challenging times. It is clear to me that if we simply move forward doing
exactly what we have been doing in the past, increasingly greater
numbers of our beloved children and their parents will come stag-
gering to our at-risk "pharmacies" in indescribable agony — begging
for pain relief.

Sunblock, anyone?

Chapter Forty

KIRUV FOR OUR CHILDREN

At the 2005 Agudath Israel National Convention, I was chairing a Project YES session where the featured speaker was my dear friend, Rabbi Noach Orlowek. Fresh off a plane from Eretz Yisrael, Reb Noach spoke brilliantly about *chinuch*, teens, and parenting matters. After his presentation, there was an extended Q&A segment with questions posed to any of the five people on the panel. At one point, Rabbi Orlowek and I were sharing the podium responding to a series of hard-hitting questions when someone got up and asked us to share with the assembled delegates our thoughts regarding how parents ought to respond to the challenges posed by the Internet. At that time, there was a great deal of discussion in the broader Orthodox community about this subject and an immediate hush passed through the audience as three hundred sets of eyes focused on Rabbi Orlowek and myself. I boldly stepped forward, firmly grabbed the microphone … and passed it to Rabbi Orlowek.

Well, Reb Noach and I are very close friends and we often kid each other about the fact that we seem to always finish each other's sentences. So, I was very curious to hear how he would reply to that loaded question.

Rabbi Orlowek was quiet for a few very long moments. He then responded by posing a question. What if a diabetic is invited to a fancy wedding where he will be surrounded with food that is terribly harmful to him? Reb Noach responded by noting that the only chance this person has to resist the temptations he will inevitably be faced with at the wedding was to see to it that he had a full and satisfying meal before he left home. Rabbi Orlowek said that we must accept the fact that each generation throughout our glorious history had its challenges and that the explosion of technology-driven temptations that our children — and we — face nowadays may very well be ours. More importantly, he pointed out that we must make peace with the fact that as much as we would like to, we simply cannot shelter our children beyond a certain age. Therefore, the only solution that we have as parents and educators is to see to it that our kids are "full" when they reach their teen years. And "full," he explained, means having an appreciation and genuine love for Torah and mitzvos; nurturing, safe, and loving home environments; schools that are welcoming and inspire children; and *rebbei'im*/teachers who develop deep and meaningful relationships with their students, in addition to teaching the timeless lessons of our Torah.

Rabbi Orlowek emphatically stated that parents must be very vigilant in protecting their vulnerable children from the corrupt and immoral content of the Internet and other media venues. However, this defensive strategy represents only one component in our quest to raise observant, Torah-committed children in these challenging times. Moreover, the shelf life of this defensive shield is limited to the time when our children are young and primarily in the confines of our homes. Once they leave the shelter of our Torah homes, they will be extremely vulnerable to the temptations they will face if we have not successfully "filled" them with a deep love of Torah and mitzvos.

I think that in the broadest sense, we ought to be thinking about fundamentally expanding the *chinuch* of our precious children. Those involved in *kiruv* (outreach) work fully understand that they need to spend a great deal of energy and time engaging the hearts and minds of the unafilliated Jews with whom they work. With our own children, however, it often seems like we mistakenly take for granted they are lifelong customers, so we fail to spend enough time in the critical arena of "customer relations." We invest an enormous amount of time filling their minds, but we often expend not nearly enough energy inspiring them and engaging their hearts.

When you think of it, what we really need are *kiruv* schools for our own children and a *kiruv* mindset in our own homes. As a wise mother once told me regarding the school experience of her children, "Rabbi Horowitz, my children need salesmen, not policemen." How true! And many of our dedicated educators truly are very effective salespeople.

Rabbi Orlowek was expressing a profound thought in his analogy of the diabetic individual. For when our beloved children enter our schools in their formative years, we are in complete control of their environment. We monitor the spiritual intake of their *neshamos* — as we well ought to. However, we must always keep in mind that these dynamics will rapidly change, as our children grow older. Like it or not, ready or not, they will be thrust into a very challenging environment where their palates will be tempted by all sorts of appealing — and harmful — products. Once that time comes, all we can do is hope and pray that we prepared them well with filling and nourishing meals.

Chapter Forty-One

ROLLING OUT THE WELCOME MAT

"We are faced with a critical problem, one that we must address as a society. There is a spiritual underclass that exists in our community — dropout teens. ... These are children that *mechanchim*, parents — indeed society as a whole — has failed to reach. In the Greater New York area there are hundreds of boys ages 16 and above who are in no yeshivah setting at all. We bump into them at the mall, and we catch sight of them through the plate-glass window of the pool hall. And their numbers are growing. Rapidly."

These lines are adapted from the first article that I published on the topic of at-risk teens, "An Ounce of Prevention," which appeared in *The Jewish Observer*, May 1996. The overriding theme of that four-thousand-word essay was that the rapidly elevated bar-to-entry at high schools was inadvertently causing significant numbers of our beloved sons and daughters to feel alienated from — and often rejected by — our school system. Here are more excerpts:

"As we ratchet up the tension level and raise the bar to encourage them to hurdle to greater heights, many of these children crash into the bar time and time again. Broken-hearted and discouraged, they simply stop trying and seek fulfillment elsewhere."

The haunting story of Elisha Ben Avuyah — Acher — comes to mind. After he had sinned, he heard a heavenly voice, which informed him that all were welcome to repent except for him. He replied, "Since the option of *teshuvah* is not available to me, I will at least derive pleasure from this world," and he *r'l* returned to his path of transgression.

These sensitive young men are misreading our well-intentioned messages to them. They are not hearing our calls to improve, they misconstrue the pleas of their parents to better their lives and enrich their futures. All that keeps reverberating in their ears is the never-ending shout of voices that pierce their hearts: "We don't want you in our classroom, in our yeshivah, in our mesivta, in our home ...."

Judging the level of the proverbial bar to entry in mesivta high schools is an inexact science at best. However, I would estimate that it is currently much higher than it was when I penned those lines, and even higher than it was when I started teaching eighth grade twenty-five years ago.

When I applied to high school in 1972, the welcome mat was out for virtually any *talmid* who wished to come. I know that to be a fact because I was accepted to the first and only school I applied to — and I was a very restless young man with a history of poor behavior. To be perfectly honest, I didn't really start learning seriously until eleventh grade. But I was given a gift that many of today's kids are denied. Time. Time to improve. Time to develop a love for learning. Time to work out whatever barriers there were to my success. Time to begin realizing my potential. Thirty-five years have a way softening the edges of difficult school experiences, but I honestly cannot recall any of my friends not getting into their high school of choice.

When you think about it, my generation, children of Holocaust-surviving parents, were given another gift by organized Judaism — unequivocal acceptance. We were all unconditionally welcomed in our schools and shuls. Our fathers and mothers didn't go to parenting classes and the vast majority of our educators didn't participate in professional development seminars. But there was a clear message that every Jewish soul was precious and treasured. Partly it was because most American Jews were assimilating, so yeshivos felt a responsibility to welcome everyone who was willing to come. Partly it was because the post-Holocaust generation could not afford to lose another Jewish soul. Whatever the reason, Jewish educators opened their doors to Jewish children.

Everywhere I go, people ask me why the "at-risk teen" crisis didn't seem to exist thirty years ago. In the past, I've offered a number of diverse theories to explain this phenomenon. Then, a few weeks ago, a frightening thought struck me. Perhaps our beloved children are mirroring our community's conditional acceptance of them with their own conditional *kabbalas mitzvos*. After all, many of our kids are increasingly getting the message that they are welcomed and valued only so long as they do well in school and do not deviate too much from our cultural norms. Our love is conditional. How would we feel if our spouse told us that he/she would love us only if we landed a great job? Would we feel that special attachment to our spouses *even if* we got the position? Who knows what harmful seeds we are sowing by having our kids jump through hoops at such a young age to get into high schools and seminaries — even for those who get accepted? Every year there are very large number of boys and girls who are not accepted in our high schools, or who have to knock on many doors before someone will grudgingly accept them.

There are no simple solutions for improving the application and vetting process for our high schools and seminaries. Not every child is an appropriate fit for every school. Parents need to be honest in assessing their children's abilities (and value the advice of their child's educators regarding placement) so as not to set their children up for repeated failure by applying to schools where their kids cannot succeed. But it is painfully clear that we educators need to put our heads together and do our very best to improve things so that *all* our children (and families) will feel cherished, valued — and wanted — in our schools and communities.

PULLING IN THE GANGPLANK

THE CUSTOMER IS
ALWAYS RIGHT ... RIGHT??

*A*lmost ten years later, I can still vividly remember the pain, confusion, and heartbreak in the eyes and voices of Yossi and his wonderful parents. When I met them, Yossi was a sincere, well-adjusted thirteen-year old *bachur*. He loved to daven and enjoyed learning *Chumash* and *Halachah*. So why had his parents called my house repeatedly, begging my wife to clear some time in my calendar to meet them? I soon found the cause of the understandable agony that Yossi and his parents were undergoing at that trying time in their lives. Over a period of a few endless weeks, Yossi had been rejected by all the mesivta high schools he had applied to. Why, you ask? Because, despite his many fine qualities, Yossi had a fatal flaw. Truth be told, Yossi was … um … er … an average boy.

Average in *Gemara*, that is. Over the course of our conversations, I found Yossi to be far above average in *middos* and *yiras Shamayim* (interpersonal relations and fear of Heaven) and flat-out superior in *mentchlichkeit* (decency and integrity.) In short, Yossi was the type of young man that we would be proud to have as a son or son-in-law.

A few months before the mesivta-application nightmare began, Yossi found a wallet in the street with over $400 in cash. Without hesitation, he returned the wallet. When the grateful owner gave him a reward, Yossi immediately gave it all to *tzedakah*! (FYI: Yossi's parents were of modest means; hence the money would have been very meaningful to him.) Yossi even wrote a beautiful letter to the *menhalim* who rejected him. He mentioned the story with the wallet, described his love for *davening*/learning, and begged to join the few mesivtos that his friends were attending. I'm sad to report that his pleas were to no avail. One *menahel* suggested that Yossi go to a school geared for weaker kids. But Yossi rightfully felt uncomfortable going there, as he had no "symptoms" — yet — of the at-risk kids who attended that school.

More than a generation ago, Rabbi Yitzchok Hutner z'tl, the revered *rosh yeshivah* of Mesivta Chaim Berlin, articulated the evolving mission of yeshivos in what was then modern-day America. He compared the *Mishkan* (Tabernacle used by the Jews during their sojourn in the desert) to the *teivah* of Noach (Noah's ark). The *Mishkan*, he said, was a place where Jews went to be inspired, to become closer to *Hashem*. Noach's *teivah*, on the other hand, was the only haven available to avoid certain death and destruction.

Rabbi Hutner explained that in pre-war Europe, yeshivos were like the *Mishkan* — places where spiritually elevated people went to grow in Torah and *yiras Shamayim*. Those who did not attend yeshivah, however, were still able to remain committed Jews, raised in the nurturing environment of the pre-war shtetel. But America is different. Due to the unraveling of the moral fabric of secular society, it was nearly impossible for a child to exist as a Torah observant Jew outside the walls of the yeshivah. American yeshivos, maintained Rabbi Hutner, were more along the lines of the *teivah* — a structure that offered shelter and protection.

It is interesting to note that while Rav Hutner's thoughts are often quoted, the context of his comments and their profound message is not as well known. Almost every time I heard this insightful quote, it was used to decry the state of today's eroded moral values. **But that is missing his main point!!** Rav Hutner was saying that we must change the way that we view our yeshivos. He was suggesting that the holy yeshivos of Volozhin and Slabodka were primarily designed for a tiny percentage of the outstanding achievers in Torah, as the grinding poverty of pre-war Europe forced the vast majority of children above the age of thirteen to join the workforce. American yeshivos and Bais Yaakovs, Rav Hutner maintained, need to be geared **for all children** to find success and refuge.

Sadly, as I alluded to in an earlier column, exactly the opposite has been happening over the past ten or fifteen years. The bar to entry at high schools in cities with large Jewish populations has become much, much higher during this period of time. The bottom line is that nowadays — with the waters of the *mabul* rising higher and higher — parental pressure has virtually forced the hands of our educators in large cities to pull in the gangplank of the *teivah* when "average" kids apply. Why? Because accepting "average" kids is the kiss of death for many schools in the eyes of the "customers," i.e., the parents of prospective applicants (that's you). The caring principals who were accepting and tolerant regarding admissions policies have had their schools relegated to second-or-third tier status by parents (that's you, again) who now shun their *mosdos*. Other school heads and board members who watched this horror show of a school's decline due to word-of-mouth unfold learn the "new math" rather quickly. The equation is quite simple and brutal. More children in these larger cities, *b'H*, means more schools in the same geographic area. More schools mean more competition. And which parent wouldn't turn over heaven and earth to get their kid accepted to the "best" schools?

How have we defined "best schools"? Obviously, those with the most rigorous entrance criteria, and those who don't accept "average" kids.

Like ... well ... Yossi.

Chapter Forty-Three

WAL-MART IS COMING

*I*magine that you were born and raised in a small farming town with a population of 5,000 people. Life was simple there, and you decided to raise your children in that rural setting. You married and shortly thereafter opened a hardware store, which, over the years, met your growing family's financial needs. You never needed to advertise or market your store much, as you had a monopoly on the hardware business in your town. After all, the closest city, and its shopping center, was 30 miles away.

Then, virtually overnight, your peaceful existence was shaken to the core when Wal-Mart announced its intention to open a mega-store 10 miles down the road from your home. You were understandably frightened, as you knew that countless mom-and-pop stores in thousands of communities across the United States went bankrupt shortly after a Wal-Mart branch opened nearby, as they were simply unable to compete with the dramatically lower prices and enhanced selection that the competition's high-volume stores offered.

The fear and uncertainty that reigned in the aftermath of the shocking news galvanized the town's residents to action. An elected official organized a meeting of all local business owners. Efforts were initiated to stall the process in court, and a letter-writing campaign to the governor asking him to thwart Wal-Mart's project was initiated. However, it was all for naught; ground was eventually broken and the ribbon-cutting ceremony for the new store was suddenly only 10 months away.

Once the inevitability of this project became apparent, you and your wife went through the classic phases of the grief cycle, along the lines of someone who had been diagnosed, *chas v'shalom*, G-d forbid, with a fatal illness:

1) Denial — This can't be happening.

2) Anger — Why is this happening?

3) Bargaining — Please don't let this happen.

4) Depression/Resignation — We are so very sad this is happening.

5) Acceptance — This is going to happen; let's deal with this challenge effectively.

Once you reached the acceptance stage (and not all do — many grieving people remain in the denial or another of the other phases), you and your fellow storeowners began planning for "life after Wal-Mart." A number of community leaders formed a committee whose mission it was to travel the country and explore how other towns responded effectively to the opening of a nearby Wal-Mart branch. While the committee was doing its due diligence, public brainstorming sessions were held weekly. All local residents were invited and many ideas to strengthen local businesses were freely discussed and considered.

One month later, the committee members returned with a mixed report. Their research indicated that Wal-Mart's imminent arrival was in fact an existential threat to their town's economic survival, as many communities they visited watched their downtown business centers turn into virtual ghost towns once Wal-Mart opened its doors. However, there were successful models to follow: cities that survived and thrived despite the threat of a Wal-Mart opening nearby. Those communities had one thing in common: they developed and executed effective, broad-based plans of action.

Inspired by the sage advice of the committee members, many initiatives were implemented that quite literally saved the town's viability. A community council was formed that began hosting events designed to build civic pride. A local legislature secured a state grant to revitalize the downtown shopping area. Pressure was exerted on the local police department to crack down and eradicate the petty street crime that plagued the business district. The mayor spearheaded an advertising campaign that highlighted the positive core values of the town. While all this was happening, a local philanthropist funded an initiative designed to help local merchants and artists sell their wares over the Internet. The results exceeded even his expectations, as quite a number of the residents developed profitable ventures over the Web. These proactive steps allowed the town to survive the onslaught of a colossal competitor and, in fact, emerge a stronger and more vibrant community. Chalk one up for the good guys.

Now for the bad news. I suggest that there are striking parallels between the Wal-Mart scenario discussed above and the state of affairs as it relates to the *chinuch* of our children in today's rapidly changing times.

You see, in the "marketplace of ideas," our Torah community was like that small town in rural America for two generations. Our children, teens, and many of our adults did almost all their intellectual shopping on our "Main Street." Sure, they were individuals who went elsewhere to browse and purchase. But they were just that, individuals.

Then, about 10 years ago, a megacompetitor came to town: the Internet. Galvanized into action, we effectively raised awareness about the dangers it poses to our children. But having Internet-free or Internet-protected homes and delaying the age when our children gain access to cell phones is only one (crucial) component of an effective policy, as this does nothing to help teens and adults deal with "Wal-Mart" once they leave the safety of our homes.

Additionally, I think that many of us are looking in the wrong direction when it comes to understanding the enormous challenge that new and evolving technology presents. Many look at the immoral content of the Internet as the primary adversary, as today's version of Yaakov Avinu's battle with the angel of Eisav. This is certainly true. The Internet and sophisticated cell phones are introducing children and adults to an onslaught of temptations and corruption. Never in history has there been so much evil so readily available and so seductively packaged. But condemnation has not solved the problem.

From my vantage point, our generation's challenge is to prepare ourselves and our children to maintain our Torah values and *hashkafos* — our fundamental beliefs — in the open arena of ideas that technology provides nowadays.

When people bemoan the challenges of the Internet to me, I silently categorize them along the lines of the five grief stages noted above:

1) Denial — *Baruch Hashem*, our teens (adults) don't use the Internet.

2) Anger — How could such a horrible thing happen to our children?

3) Bargaining — Let's daven that the Internet does not cause more kids to go off the *derech*. [I would like to point out that this is a most appropriate response. However, just as

Yaakov Avinu prepared for Eisav in three ways — with a gift, with *tefillah*, and with a battle plan — so too, *tefillah* is an important component of a multipronged approach. But we cannot rely on *tefillah* alone to address this existential threat to our *mesorah*.]

4) Depression/Resignation — The [challenges presented by the] Internet is a *gezeirah*, an edict from Heaven, and it is so very sad that we are losing so many kids because of it. But what can we do besides keep it out of our homes?

5) Acceptance — The Internet is here to stay; let's continue to shield our homes and children as best we can. But at the same time, we must deal with this incredible challenge effectively as possible.

I do not have the time or the inclination to conduct a study of which one of the five stages is most commonly cited by people who speak to me; but I would say that denial is by far the most frequent, followed by depression, bargaining, acceptance, and anger.

We are running out of time. We must develop a coherent, multiphased approach to these unprecedented challenges. The phenomenon of off-the-*derech* teens and adults who are, "All Dressed Up With Nowhere to Go" is just the beginning. Wal-Mart is coming. In fact, it has already opened its doors — and is planning to expand.

Are we prepared to deal with it effectively and protect our children — and adults — from it?

CHAPTER FORTY-FOUR

ALL DRESSED UP WITH NOWHERE TO GO

O.T.H.D. AND O.T.D.

*B*y now, we are all familiar with the condition known as "ADD" – an acronym for Attention Deficit Disorder. In the broadest sense, it reflects the difficulty or inability of an individual to sustain the level of concentration necessary to function properly: in school, at work, or in other arenas of social interaction.

Although the term most often bandied around in regard to this disorder is ADD, the type of attention deficit that is most recognizable is actually ADHD – the "bouncy" type – with the additional letter 'H' representing the hyperactivity component. Children and adults with ADHD fidget, squirm, and often interrupt others during conversations. They are also far more likely to be high-energy individuals, optimistic, charming, and generally fun to be with.

ADD, (without the letter "H") is commonly known as the "Inattentive Type." Youngsters and adults who have ADD without the hyperactivity are pleasant people to be around but are forgetful and seem to be daydreamers. However, since high-profile hyperactivity is not present in their form of attention deficit, they don't draw attention to themselves, and often slip through the cracks, undiagnosed and untreated.

If you think about it, there is a similar duality of sorts as it pertains to the off-the-*derech* phenomenon. I classify them as OTHD and OTD — off-the-*derech* with hyperactivity and off-the-*derech* without the hyperactivity.

We are all familiar with the OTHD profile. These are the off-the-*derech* youngsters who attract our attention with their hyperactivity. They engage in high-profile rebellious acts such as hard drinking/drug use, drop out of school, or dress in ways that defy our communal norms. But there is a parallel, rapidly growing off-the-*derech* phenomenon that is unnoticed and unaddressed – the OTD kind without the hyperactivity. These are youngsters who are just going through the motions in our schools and public spaces, but are not spiritually connected to our Torah.

I am getting a new wave of parents begging me to speak to their children. The profile is chillingly similar: 13-14-year-old boys and girls, high achievers, well adjusted, with no emotional problems. They just don't want to be *frum*. Period. They are eating on Yom Kippur, not keeping Shabbos, not keeping kosher, et al. No anger, no drugs, no immoral activity. They have simply rejected *Yiddishkeit*. Some have decided to "go public," while others are still going through the motions of mitzvah observance. In some cases, their educators have no idea what is really going on, as many of the children are consistently scoring well on their Hebrew and General Studies tests.

Rabbis Mordechai Becher and Chanan (Antony) Gordon wrote about a similar phenomenon occurring with *frum* adults in their excellent "Adults at Risk" article in *The Jewish Observer*. They discussed meeting *frum* adults who had significant *emunah* questions that had been suppressed and therefore had not been addressed in their formative years. Many felt spiritually and educationally unprepared for their inevitable encounter with the secular world, while they had been presented with a negative view of non-Jewish people that was disproved by their own experiences in the workplace. Both these situations caused individuals to start to question the lessons they had been taught in their yeshivah years. The writers aptly described these adults as "all dressed up with nowhere to go," meaning that they possessed all the external trappings of observant Jews but were spiritually hollow.

Are these "OTD-without-the-hyperactivity" children isolated blips on the radar screen or are they ominous signs of a growing trend? Only time will tell. But as much as I hope for the former, from my vantage point, it is starting to feel more like the latter. In the past four months, I received about 10 calls at home from parents whose children fit the profile that I described above, and our Project Y.E.S. office received an additional five calls of this nature. Projecting by using these basic numbers, try to calculate how many youngsters like that are in our school systems. This is a new and frightening experience for me, even after 25 years of working with at-risk youngsters. I have some very strong thoughts regarding why this is happening. Suffice it to say, this is cause for great concern.

Addressing this "OTD-without-the-hyperactivity" phenomenon head-on will take courage – real courage, because this issue will not be solved by creating more at-risk schools and/or programs. To proactively reverse this trend, we will need to fine-tune the way we transmit our precious *mesorah* to all our children.

Chapter Forty-Five

BUILDING A LIFE ON QUICKSAND

I recently received a riveting email from a bachur vividly describing his home life and the challenge that it posed to his emotional development. Here are his actual comments, which I edited for publication. Reading these lines reminded me of the words of our great rebbi, Rabbi Avrohom Pam, who would often remark that the formula for success with one's children is 50% tefila — prayer, and 50% shalom bayis — marital harmony.

The feelings of shame and guilt started when I was a little child. My parents didn't express any joy at being with each other. They criticized each other harshly, and they always found something to criticize about me. My parents would argue in my presence in loud voices, often yelling at each other in anger. Terrified of what might happen, I would withdraw to stunned silence. When I was finally able to speak, I would plead with them to stop fighting, but each wanted to justify him or herself in my eyes – which seemed to me as if they were expecting me to solve their problems.

I would desperately want to cry during those times. However, the only people who could have consoled me — my parents — were actually frightening me to death. I knew that I had to find a way to get my Mommy and Tatty back, because I needed them to reassure me that everything was all right, to calm me down from my terror. So I began to live my entire life trying to make people think I was good, hoping that I would stop feeling ashamed — feelings that were, of course, extremely painful. I became the perfect student who always got high marks, and the ideal child who always behaved and did his chores. Over the years, I received many, many compliments for the good things I did but, since they were all addressed to the "fake me," they did not make me feel any better. The "real me" was still riddled with shame.

If only my parents had seen my pain then, when I was a little kid who needed soothing. If only they would have realized that their bickering and fighting were making my life miserable, and that destroying their beloved child's happiness was far too high a price to pay for winning an argument. Perhaps then they would have stopped and made peace with each other, so that together they could have focused on their vulnerable little boy who needed his Mommy and Tatty so much. Maybe then, they could have been at my side to help me grow up a happy and healthy individual. Maybe then I would not have lived with such deep shame and loneliness for so many years, thinking I had been forsaken by everyone — certain that nobody cared about me.

When I tell my mother now that I had a tough time as a teenager, she is shocked and disappointed that I never shared anything with her about my feelings. She deeply regrets not having been able to give me the support I needed. My father tries so hard to make me happy now, and he also cares about me, but I never shared anything with him either. I am currently a "regular" yeshiva bachur of

19 following a traditional, acceptable path, although I didn't ever receive the kind of outside support that I needed. Ironically, if I had *chas veshalom* gone off the Torah path, I probably would have received a lot more attention and support. Baruch Hashem, I now have found people who are giving me support and guidance. I speak to therapists and to my sister to whom I feel close, and they tell me I am really a good person, and that I should focus on all the good that I do. I wish I could do that, but this is not something I can switch on at will. Now and then I feel hopeful that maybe I will change, and that gives me the courage to continue. I am also beginning to see that there are people who care about me, and that I am not all bad. I am starting to think that maybe, just maybe, I deserve to be happy and to be cared for.

I am so lonely, and I wish I could get married to someone who will be my friend. I keep thinking about my parents' lives and their marriage, and I am petrified that I will repeat the unstable environment in which I spent my painful childhood years. So I am working on changing the way I feel, in order to prepare to start a healthy home of my own.

Parents, please take a good look at your children. Somewhere there is a little boy or girl who is wondering why his/her Mommy and Tatty sometimes just leave him/her alone with his/her pain, as if he/she does not deserve to be held when he/she cries. If you do not act now, then later nothing you do will make a difference, and you will have to helplessly watch your teenager struggle with more pain than he can possibly carry on his young shoulders. Just ask my parents how it feels to know you have been unable to help your child with the struggles of growing up. Ask them how it feels to know that they were the cause of my struggles. Please realize that when you are in conflict with your spouse, you are taking away your kid's Mommy and Tatty. Realize it now, before it is too late.

Chapter Forty-Six

A CLINICAL ANALYSIS

ON *BUILDING A LIFE ON QUICKSAND*

*he previous column focused on a searing letter that I re-
ceived from a 19-year-old bachur vividly describing his
stressful home life and the challenges that it posed to his emotional development.*

*In order to enable our readers to gain a perspective on this
letter through the eyes of a mental health professional, I asked
Dr. Benzion Sorotzkin, an outstanding clinical psychologist, to
share with our readers his analysis of the bachur's letter – and
its ramifications for all parents. Here are his comments:*

The *bachur*'s letter describing his struggle growing up in a home
with no *shalom bayis* touched me deeply. While I have, obviously,

always known that the lack of parental *shalom bayis* deeply wounds children, reading the heart-felt, eloquent words from the victim himself really brought the message home.

Common sense would suggest that children who are exposed to parental conflict over a prolonged period of time would get used to it. But many studies show that this is not the case. The reason for this is because children's exposure to parental conflict increases their feelings of emotional insecurity, thus decreasing their capacity for regulating emotions and behavior, leaving them more prone to feelings of fear, distress and anger.

In fact, there is overwhelming research and clinical evidence regarding the association between chronic marital conflict and children's adjustment difficulties. There are numerous factors, such as the child's temperament and the specific circumstances of each situation, which will shape each child's response to parental conflict. For example, the degree of **perceived threat** (the extent to which children believe that the conflict will escalate, result in harm to oneself or to other family members, or threaten the family's existence), and **self-blame** (the degree to which children hold themselves personally responsible for parents' quarrels) are all important factors in shaping children's internal and external reactions to parental conflict. Children who are pulled into their parent's conflict are at risk of becoming targets of parental hostility, which might heighten perception of threat.

Parents often exacerbate the negative impact of their conflicts on their children by actually telling them that they are responsible for the parental conflict, and by undermining their children's confidence in their own coping skills by constantly criticizing them.

A serious obstacle to helping children deal with parents who lack *shalom bayis* is the pervasive denial common among both parents and their children regarding the seriousness of the marital conflict. Even when the therapist uncovers a picture of serious spousal conflict, including verbal and physical aggression (it is important to note that parents who are abusive to their spouses are also likely to be abusive to their children), the parents will confirm the details but will vigorously dispute the characterization suggested by the therapist (i.e., a home with no *shalom bayis*). "No one has a perfect marriage!" they will protest, as if a loveless and hostile marriage is equivalent to a good and loving, but imperfect, marriage. The denial becomes particularly strident if someone suggests that the child's difficulty may have something to do with the conflicted and hostile environment he grew up in.

Ironically, the same parents who very readily blame their children's negative behaviors on the influence of bad friends or an inadequate teacher will bristle at the suggestion that their children's development is strongly influenced by the home environment they grew up in. No one protests when parents are complimented for their role in their children's successes, but many will react with indignation if lack of success is also attributed to home influences. Many in our community are very eager to attribute teenagers' deviant behaviors to the power of outside influences, such as Internet – but react with accusations of "parent bashing" if the suggestion is made that parental conflict may play a decisive role.

Let us return to the *bachur's* letter and where the theme of shame that permeates his comments. Research and clinical evidence indicate that when parents are unable or unwilling to be attuned to their children's emotional and developmental needs, they create fertile grounds for the development of pervasive shameful feelings. This is especially true if children are a focus of parental conflict and certainly when they are the targets of chronic criticism. The child develops the unconscious feeling that his unmet developmental yearnings are manifestations of a loathsome defect or an inherent inner badness. The *bachur's* reactions of emotionally withdrawing and trying to stop his parents' fighting are both typical reactions. He also clearly articulates the horrible dilemma of children whose parents induce terrible fear in them, especially because, sadly, these children are now unable to turn to the very people *Hashem* designated to give them solace, comfort and reassurance.

The *bachur's* reaction to the shame by trying to become perfect and by developing a "false self," as well as his fear of marriage are, sad to say, common and very understandable reactions to his experiences.

I am glad to read that he has at last found people who are providing him with the support that his parents never seemed to be able give him. One can only hope that all parents who read his letter take his heartfelt plea seriously in order to avoid these preventable tragedies.

Dr. Sorotzkin can be reached at (718) 377-6408 or via email at bensort@aol.com.

SOURCES

Cummings, E. M. & Davies, P. T. Effects of Marital Conflict on Children: Recent Advances and Emerging Themes in Process-Oriented Research. Journal of Child Psychology and Psychiatry, 2002, Vol. 43 (1), pp. 31-63.

Davies, P. T. & Cummings, E. M. Marital Conflict and Child Adjustment: An Emotional Security Hypothesis. Psychological Bulletin, 1994, Vol. 116 (3), pp. 387-411.

Gerard, J. M., Buehler, C., Franck, K., & Anderson, O. In the Eyes of the Beholder: Cognitive Appraisals as Mediators of the Association Between Interparental Conflict Youth Maladjustment. Journal of Family Psychology, 2005, Vol. 19 (3), pp. 376-384.

Grych, J. H. & Fincham, F. D. Children's Appraisals of Marital Conflict: Initial Investigations of the Cognitive-

Contextual Framework. Child Development, 1993, Vol. 64 (1), pp. 215-230.

Morrison, A. P. & Stolorow, R. D. Shame, Narcissism, and Intersubjectivity. In M. R. Lansky & A. P. Morrison (Eds.), The Widening Scope of Shame (pp. 63-87). 1997, Hillsdale, NJ: The Analytic Press.

Sorotzkin, B. Understanding and Treating Perfectionism in Religious Adolescents. Psychotherapy, 1998, Vol. 35, pp. 87-85. [An edited version is available at www.DrSorotzkin.com]

ALL ALONE ... AGAIN

REFLECTIONS ON TISHAH B'AV 5766

Eichah yashvah vadad — Alas, she sits in solitude (*Eichah* 1:1). The haunting words of *Megillas Eichah* resonate in our hearts and minds as we sit on the ground commemorating the destruction of the *Beis Hamikdash* 1,938 years ago.

Sadly, history is repeating itself once again. Our brothers and sisters in Eretz Yisrael are being subjected to devastating destruction and terror as about 100 rockets per day rain down on them. A sea of enemies surrounds us. The leader of Iran has once again called for the eradication *r'l* of Israel, and has publicly stated that, "Israel's destruction is the solution [to the conflict]." The vile, hate-filled, anti-Semitic rhetoric emanating from many leaders in the

Arab world and from most of the Arab media is at least equivalent to that of the Nazi propaganda machine in the late 1930's. The vast majority of nations would deny us the right to protect **our** women and children by any means possible. It is hard to avoid the feeling that *Klal Yisrael* is isolated and alone … again.

So what does this mean for us? How are we, who live in comfort and security in America, to respond to the unfolding tragedy in Eretz Yisrael? After reading the *haftaros* of The Three Weeks and the poignant words of *Megillas Eichah*; after reflecting on the *kinos* we just recited — what are the messages we ought to internalize?

We all know that we ought to increase our *tefillos*, and we are. We all know that we need to share the burden with our brothers and sisters in Eretz Yisrael, and we are — in many ways. This week, I received e-mails from two parents in Yeshiva Darchei Noam, where I serve as *menahel*. They are both members of the local volunteer fire corps and they independently decided to travel to Eretz Yisroel in order to assist the overworked Israeli firefighters battling the many blazes caused by the barrage of rockets.

But how can we honestly relate to the agony of the hundreds of thousands of our brothers and sisters living in the northern portions of Eretz Yisrael — Tzfas, Haifa, etc. — who have been rendered homeless and unemployed due to incessant and deadly rocket attacks? How can we honestly relate to the sheer terror — and bravery — of the parents of Israeli soldiers who are in active combat in Southern Lebanon or Gaza? We, who become anxious when our adult children are driving on the highways in thunderstorms, how can we relate to the sleepless nights that these parents must be undergoing?

So, what are we to do? I guess I would divide the "take-aways" in two groups:

Offer material and emotional support to our brothers and sisters in Eretz Yisrael. Especially now, with the advent of the Internet, there is so much you can do. Purchase items online in Israeli stores. Send e-mails of support to your relatives in Eretz Yisrael. Support the organizations that are helping our brothers and sisters in Eretz Yisrael. Daven *for* the soldiers who are risking their lives to protect our brothers and sisters.

Adopt a family, community or school. Last September, our yeshivah adopted the elementary school of Atzmonah, Gush Katif, that was relocated to the Netivot area. We bought school supplies, sports equipment, and for Pesach, we partnered with a *chesed* organization and bought each of the students a brand-new bicycle. Our children and theirs exchanged letters and cards throughout the year. It was so much appreciated by them — and so rewarding for my *talmidim*.

On a more personal and spiritual note; I think we all ought to read the stirring and timeless words of our *nevi'im* in the *haftaros* of *Shabbos Chazon* and Tishah B'av — and make a sincere *cheshbon hanefesh*. There are two recurring themes in these lines. One relates to the Jews of those times serving idols and forsaking Hashem. That, however, at least on the surface, is not very relevant today. The second theme, on the other hand, is very much germane to our lives. It addresses the fact that the Jews of those times were concentrating on spiritual trappings (bringing *korbanos*) and not on the essence of Hashem's Torah (honesty, integrity, and kindness).

"Why do I need your numerous sacrifices?" (*Yeshayah* 1:11), asks *Hashem*. The *navi* exclaims that *Hashem* is "weary of your *korbanos*" (1:14), and that He "will not listen to your prayers" (1:15). Why was that so? It was certainly a great mitzvah to purchase and bring *korbanos* to the *Beis Hamikdash*. But, as the *navi* relates, those mitzvos were mere adornments to the core values of our Torah. And the *navi* clearly describes what the Jews needed to do in order to redeem themselves. "Purify yourselves, seek justice, strengthen the victim, and take up the cause of the widow/orphan (1:16-17)."

I suggest that we engage in a constructive *cheshbon hanefesh* regarding the essential elements of the qualities noted by the *Navi* — honesty, integrity, true *ahavas Yisrael*, supporting those among us who are weak and unable to conduct their lives with *simchas hachayim*. We should be asking ourselves if we are doing all we can to make a true *Kiddush Hashem* in our interactions with non-Jews, non-religious Jews, and *frum Yidden* who may be of different backgrounds. For these qualities is the essence of what Hashem's Torah produces.

In these troubling times, when we are surrounded by our enemies, isolated and alone, we ought to be striving to fulfill the timeless charge of Yirmiyahu in the closing words of today's *haftarah*, "For only with this may one glorify himself; become wise and [get to] know Me [contemplate how to better emulate the ways of Hashem], for I am *Hashem* who does kindness, justice, and righteousness ...." (*Yirmiyahu* 9:23).

May *Hashem* dry our tears and comfort us with the rebuilding of the *Beis Hamikdash*.

BASIC
TRAINING

MEMORIES OF RABBI SHERER *Z'TL*

There was almost a surreal feeling in the nearly deserted ball-room of the New York Hilton as Rabbi Shmuel Bloom met with the staff of Agudas Yisrael after the 76th Annual Dinner to plan for the *levayah* of Rabbi Sherer. Exhausted from the demands of the dinner, and emotionally drained from the crushing blow of Rabbi Sherer's *petirah* only hours earlier, the staff set aside their emotions and focused on the countless details necessary to insure that the proper *kavod acharon* would be given.

The staff. For the past few months, I have been privileged to be part of this illustrious group of multitalented men and women handpicked by Rabbi Sherer to serve the *klal* in such a dignified manner. I sat quietly throughout the meeting, watching as every one of the myriad details of the *levayah* was discussed. How ironic it was that the well-oiled machine that under the watchful eye of Rabbi Sherer produced so many events that created such *kevod Shamayim* would now be engaged to provide the *kavod acharon* for him.

Throughout the meeting, I watched as members of the staff would pause for a moment, as if to step back and reflect on the *petirah* of Rabbi Sherer. A soft sigh would escape, and then the thought, "We have a job to do," would clearly come to mind, and the person would plunge back to the work at hand.

Although most of the others had spent decades with Rabbi Sherer, and quite literally felt as if their father had passed away, I felt a different sense of loss. I was envious of the others for having had the training from Rabbi Sherer that was so evident in everything that they do. Having been recently appointed to head a new endeavor that is rich with so much promise and fraught with so much danger, I felt almost cheated at the thought of not having his guidance.

A story I had heard years ago came to mind.

Approximately 40 years ago, an esteemed member of the Yerushalmi *Kehillah* was on his deathbed. His entire extended family surrounded him as the end came closer. Knowing that he had moments to live, he turned to his children and remarked that there are many thoughts that he would like to share with them, but, *"Ich hub moira fun p'neyos"* (He was concerned that it would be a smattering of boastfulness for him to assume that he was in a position to give direction to others). He recited the *Shema*, and passed from this world without sharing his thoughts with anyone.

His children were inconsolable at their lost opportunity to hear the thoughts and guidance that their father had initially wanted to share with them. When Reb Shmuel Shapiro z'tl, one of the elders of the *Kehillah,* came to be *menachem avel,* one of the sons expressed his feelings of grief to Reb Shmuel. Reb Shmuel was silent for a moment. He then softly said in Yiddish, "But he did give you *guidance.* He taught you the importance of conducting yourself with *tzeniyus* and humility.

I had received my guidance all right. I wasn't paying enough attention.

My training began on my first day in the Agudah office with a two-hour meeting with Rabbi Shmuel Bloom, as he — with great passion — outlined the ideals and goals of Agudas Yisrael. "People don't fully understand the goal of Reb Meir Shapiro with the Daf Hayomi. It was not just a program to spread *limud hatorah.* It was the best way to unite *Klal Yisroel.* That is the mission of Agudas Yisrael."

Rabbi Sherer dropped in for a few minutes to wish me *mazel tov.* He returned a few moments later with a beautifully inscribed copy of *Against All Odds.* "Read it carefully, Reb Yakov," he said, "and learn about Agudas Yisrael." He spoke to me for a few moments. As he stood up to leave the room, he placed a hand on my shoulder, and said "As a *rebbi,* you were able to touch 25 lives a year — perhaps 1000 lives over your teaching career. Working for Agudas Yisrael, you can help all of *Klal Yisrael.* I trust that you can meet that challenge."

Throughout my first few months with Agudas Yisrael, I was initiated into the philosophy of the Agudah movement — commitment to helping fellow *Yidden,* fidelity to *Gedolei Torah,* and the incredible sense of *achdus* and backing from the lay people who are the backbone of the organization.

My personal *tzava'ah* would come several months later.

Two weeks before the *petirah* of Rabbi Sherer, I got a call from his personal secretary regarding an ad for the Project Y.E.S. parenting workshops that appeared in the newspaper that week. "Rabbi Sherer asked you to please make the following corrections to the ad before you run it again," she said.

"You did not include cross streets in the ad. The ad read that the sessions will be conducted at Rabbi Reisman's *shul* at 2122 Ave S. The cross streets (i.e., between East 21st and East 22nd streets) should be included. People who don't live in Flatbush, may not know exactly where the *shul* is located.

"The ad read: Rabbi Horowitz has been conducting parenting sessions … over the past few years. Rabbi Sherer said that if his memory is correct, you first spoke at the 1996 Agudas Yisroel National Convention. That means you probably weren't doing much public speaking until then.

"Take out the word *few;* instead the text should say over the past years."

"At the bottom of the ad there was a note stating that 'all proceeds — there was an entrance fee of $10 per couple — will benefit Project Y.E.S.'

"Add the word exclusively. Since all the money is going to the Agudah, it should state that fact clearly."

She paused for a moment, and added, "Rabbi Sherer asked me to tell you that Agudas Yisrael is the organization that it is, because he personally checked every ad and every letter that we sent out for the past 50 years."

In one minute, I got my orders that would have to last for a lifetime. Guide people as much as you possibly can. Examine every word you speak or write for absolute honesty. And above all, be forthright about the finances of charity projects.

My first reaction was one of great *simchah*. Having heard how deathly ill Rabbi Sherer was, I mistakenly took that phone call to be a sign that he was feeling better. I turned on my computer, typed a short memo, and faxed it to Rabbi Sherer's home. I thanked him for the corrections, and then added a postscript. "Let me join *Klal*

Yisrael in wishing you a refuah sheleimah. May we be zocheh to have *your eina pekicha* (watchful eye) *biz a hundret un tzvontzik."*

Lo zachinu. Lo zachinu.

THE FORTUNATE ONES

*I*n the spring of 1997 I received a phone call from Rabbi Dovid Bernstein, head of *Torah Umesorah's Aish Dos* program. He invited me to join a group of 17 *menahalim* (principals) who were participating in a newly formed three-year Senior Leadership Program. I would need to devote three weeks during each of the following three summers, travel to *Eretz Yisrael*, and attend classes and lectures delivered by leading educators. It sounded like a great prospect – for someone else.

After 15 years of teaching eighth-grade *talmidim*, I was about to pursue my dream of opening a yeshivah, and I didn't think that I could spare three days, let alone three weeks. And, to be perfectly honest, I was a bit skeptical as to the possible benefit of such a program. Still, I allowed Reb Dovid to convince me to join the program. "Come along, Reb Yakov," he said. ' It will change your life."

Well, *Baruch Hashem* I did — and it did.

It is difficult in these few lines to convey what this program did for me – and my colleagues. Over the course of the next three years, we were exposed to the greatest minds in the world of *chinuch* – with opportunities to discuss the issues and challenges we face on a daily basis with our *gedolim shlita*. We were encouraged to evaluate our teaching practices, and to explore innovative techniques that would enhance the learning of our *talmidim* and *talmidos*. We spent many hours developing our skills and learning to better articulate the vision and mission of our *mosdos*.

We all grew together, individually, and as a cohesive group. Perhaps the greatest long-term benefit for us was the fact that the 17 *menahalim* from around the country, representing *mosdos* ranging from *chassidishe* yeshivos to out-of-town day schools – became an incredibly close-knit group who continue to contact each other regularly, and to exchange curriculum materials and share ideas and innovative programs.

Over the past 10 years, I have been watching the *rebbei'im* of our yeshivah experience the thrill of professional growth at the annual Torah Umesorah conventions. A Torah Umesorah convention is so much more than merely the sum of its parts: the incredible range of topics in the dozens of practical and educational workshops; several rooms brimming with classroom materials culled from the files of outstanding *mechanchim* and *mechanchos* from around the world; the Friday Morning Networking Breakfast, during which *mechanchim* are able to share ideas with their colleagues.

Devoting one's life to *chinuch* is not merely a career choice, but a mission, an answer of a call to a higher duty. In today's materialistic society, the forgoing of potentially lucrative careers to dedicate oneself to the mission of Hashem is the quintessential act of true *mesiras nefesh*. It is therefore so important for our *mechanchim* and *mechanchos* to have the opportunity to spend Shabbos with our leading *gedolim* and hear their much-appreciated *divrei brachah* and *chizuk*. In fact, my great *rebbi*, Rabbi Avrohom Pam *z'tl*, often spent a major portion of his yearly address at the Torah Umesorah convention giving encouragement to my colleagues who serve as *menhalim* and *rebbei'im* in smaller, out-of-town communities, where the challenges are much greater.

In the years when I have had the good fortune to attend Torah Umesorah conventions, I often look around during *Kabbalas Shabbos*, as more than 1,000 *mechanchim daven* together in an indescribable display of *avodah shebelev* (service of the heart). I feel so fortunate to be part of this illustrious group of *shluchei d'Rachmona* (emissaries of Hashem).

Ashreinu. Mah tov chelkeinu. Mah na'im goraleinu — How fortunate we are! How good is our portion! How pleasant is our lot!

Chapter Fifty

THANK YOU, ALL

The story is told of a financial analyst who had his head near a raging fire and his legs in an ice bucket. When asked how he was feeling, he responded that on the average he is doing just fine.

Sometimes, I feel like that poor fellow.

I write two types of columns: uplifting *divrei Torah* on the *parashah*[1] and parenting columns that often highlight the areas in our society that are in need of improvement. Week after week, Sundays through Tuesdays, I turn on my laptop, and work on my columns, usually in the predawn hours. I use my *sefarim* and keyboard to do my best to inspire teens — and their parents — by crafting a positive message from the weekly Torah portion. I also

---

1. My dvar Torah sefer, "Growing With the Parsha – Torah Thoughts for Teens," can be purchased by emailing admin@rabbihorowitz.com or by calling 845-352-7100 x 133.

utilize that block of time to shine light on the darker corners of our society, and I offer solutions to remediate some of these communal problems that we would prefer were not there.

But I guess that is the way it should be. Torah should inspire us. And we should seek to improve our lives. *Hashem* and our Torah are perfect. We are not flawless — yet.

I often think, however, that regular readers of my parenting lines may be left with an inaccurately negative perception of our Torah society. Over the past few months, I have been thinking about taking a week off from the doom-and-gloom-teen-crisis mode in order to write a column that celebrates what is wonderful and outstanding in our world. Somehow, however, I never got around to writing that one.

Until now.

A few weeks ago, on a quiet Shabbos morning, one of my family members had an urgent medical condition that required us to rush to the local hospital. *Baruch Hashem*, it turned out to be very temporary in nature, and things were back to normal by the afternoon. All day long, my grandmother's words kept coming to mind, *"Ribbono Shel Olam; shrek mich, nor shtruf mich nisht."* Loosely translated, it means, "Master of the World, go ahead and frighten me [in the context of a medical emergency], but please do not punish me [with things that are permanent in nature].

For eight hours, I was in a very rare state of suspended animation in an emergency waiting room. No cell phone, no laptop, no one to talk to when my family member was sedated and napping. And, once it became clear that there was nothing medically significant, I was left sitting in a straight-backed, plastic chair — with a great deal of time on my hands to reflect in silence.

As the day wore on, I kept thinking of the amazing acts of selflessness and *chesed* that I had been witnessing all day — and how very proud I am to be a *frum* Jew.

We called *Hatzolah* at 7:40 on a quiet, sunny Shabbos morning. Two young men were at our home within 60 seconds. Cheerful, competent and professional, they took care of the medical issues at hand and comforted their patient throughout the ride to the hospital. Once we were settled, they left, only to return with another patient within a half-hour. Over the next three hours, they made FIVE trips to the hospital, with the same good-natured, wisecracking — but serious — composure.

Since, I had no food with me, I was directed to the Bikur Cholim Refrigerator, where I was able to make *Kiddush* and grab a bite. I was never able to thank the volunteers who lovingly prepared the wrapped packets of cake and cookies, or the owners of the bakeries and grocery stores who donated the food and drink that stocked the shelves. During the eight hours that we were in the hospital, we were visited by numerous Bikur Cholim volunteers, who walked four miles in 90-degree heat to give much-needed comfort to hospital patients and their family members.

Around noontime, there was a lull in the action in our hospital room. I walked over to the new Bikur Cholim Shabbos Home, located right near the hospital. A friend of mine who wishes to remain anonymous purchased and renovated it for the use of family members who remain near the hospital on Shabbos and Yom Tov. I had to blink back tears as I took a self-led tour of the home, which was so thoughtfully and tastefully set up. Everything was spotless and freshly painted. There was fresh, matching linen on the beds. The kitchen was fully stocked — from soup to nuts, quite literally. I could have had a full meal or any type of snack. There were *sefarim*, Jewish newspapers, and games for kids to play. A beautiful deck was recently built off the kitchen area to afford the guests some moments of relaxation when the weather would permit it. The house was empty when I visited it, but there were signs of significant use. Three cars were parked in the driveway, two with out-of-state license plates.

Throughout the remaining hours that we spent in the hospital, I kept thinking of the things that we take for granted: our health, for example. Sitting in a hospital room for a few hours gives a person a better perspective on why our *chachamim* included daily *berachos* in our morning prayers: to remind us that we need to thank Hashem each and every day for our health and well-being.

On a communal level, as well, there is so much that we should appreciate. We should be celebrating our success at transmitting our eternal Torah values to our children. We should be so very proud of the respect that our children have for their elders, about the fact that so many *mechanchim* and *mechanchos* devote their lives, year after year, to educate and inspire our children in yeshivos and Bais Yaakovs across this country. We should pause and take stock of the galaxy of *gemach* organizations (free loan and charitable volunteer groups) in our communities, to which countless numbers of our friends devote their time and energy helping their neighbors. We should appreciate the devotion and communal responsibility of those in our community who have achieved financial success, and recognize the personal sacrifices that they make and they can hardly eat a meal without being disturbed by those in need of their assistance. And we should be grateful to *Hashem* for the amazing groups of decent, spiritual, and idealistic friends that our children have.

So, next week, I guess that I will continue with my *divrei Torah* and my parenting columns. I will try to inspire — and do my best to point out areas where we need to improve.

But, for just this week, please allow me to use these lines in order to pause and thank all of you who helped make my Shabbos morning less stressful:

To the Hatzolah dispatcher who took my call politely and professionally.

To the Hatzolah members who did such a marvelous job helping my family member.

To your spouses and children who graciously share your time and love with Klal Yisrael.

To the Bikur Cholim volunteers who visited us, to those who lovingly stocked the shelves, who prepared the kugels and cholent, who painted the walls and cleaned the rooms in the Shabbos home.

To the Bikur Cholim and Echo medical-referral staff members for being available 24/7 to assist and reassure those of us who must make instant and critical medical decisions for which we are unprepared (I did not make use of your services this time, but it was a great source of comfort to me to know that I could have).

To the countless members of the support staffs of these wonderful organizations, and to those who run the fund-raisers without which none of this work would be possible.

And to those who anonymously contribute the funds that enable these wonderful organizations to do their lifesaving work.

To all of you, on behalf of my family members, I offer my humble thanks, and my sincere tefillos:

May the Ribbono Shel Olam reward you for your countless, selfless acts of kindness.

May He protect you from harm as you engage in your holy and lifesaving work.

May you always be able to give — and never need anyone's assistance.

With boundless gratitude,
Yakov Horowitz

Afterword

This book is dedicated in loving memory of my dear father, Reb Shlomo Horowitz *a'h*, and, *yibodel l'chaim tovim*, in honor of my dear parents, Shlomo and Beile Nutovic.

My father *a'h* was born in 1922 to his parents, Reb Yakov Moshe and Leah Gittel (nee Katz) Horowitz in Ihel, Rumania. His formative years were spent in the loving embrace of his extended family, led by his paternal grandfather, Reb Dov Berish Horowitz, affectionately known throughout Hungary and Rumania as "Reb Berish Vishever." Reb Berish faithfully served as *chazzan* and *shochet* in that community for over fifty years, and wrote *niggunim* (songs) for many *Admorim* and *Rebbei'im* in his region, many of which are still sung in Chassidic courts today.

When his father, Reb Yakov Moshe (for whom I am named) moved to Scranton, Pennsylvania with his wife and children in the early 1930's, my father remained behind with his paternal grandparents and learned in the local yeshivah until 1938, when, with war clouds gathering, he used his priceless American passport provided by my grandfather to join his family in the USA.

Tragically, his grandparents, Reb Berish and Rochel Miriam (nee Taub, cousin of Rabbi Yecheskel Landau *z'tl*, later known as the Veretsky Rov of Flatbush), his other eight children and many dozens of their grandchildren and great-grandchildren, were all killed *al Kiddush Hashem* in the *gehenom* of Auchwitz, *h'yd*. (See "My Grandfather and I" (p.167). Of all the four generations of Reb Berish and Rochel Miriam's descendants, only Reb Yakov Moshe and his children: Shirley Ganz (Scranton), my father *a'h*, Esther Ehrman (Washington Heights and later Bnei Braq), Brenda Eichler Moschytz (Baltimore and later Yerushalayim), Rabbi Ahron Hersch (Herschel) Horowitz *a'h* (Scranton), Dr. David (Duddy) Horowitz (Scranton) and Reb Sholem Horowitz (Philadelphia) survived the war years.

My father attended Yeshivah Torah Vodaas, was apprenticed as a diamond cutter/trader, and later married my mother, Beile, daughter of Moshe Dovid and Sara (nee Perl) Ganz of Newburgh, New York. The Ganz family, coincidently, also hailed from Vishevus, Rumania, and was close to the Horowitz family in Europe. In fact, my mother's eldest brother, Reb Herschel (Harry) Ganz *a'h*, of Scranton, Pennsylvania, actually sang in the choir of my great-grandfather Reb Berish alongside my father *a'h*, who would later become his brother-in-law.

Reb Moshe Dovid and Sara Ganz, my maternal grandparents, strived mightily to raise their children as observant Jews in a city where there were many hundreds of formerly frum families who abandoned Yiddishkeit en masse upon coming to America. When she arrived in America, Sara Ganz sold one of her most valuable and prized possessions — her expensive down winter coat — to procure the funds necessary to send her two teenage sons, Harry and Sam, to Yeshivah Torah Vodaas. She was instrumental in raising her two daughters, Goldie (Diamond) and my mother Beile as proud Torah Jews. Moshe Dovid and Sara accomplished something almost unheard of in those times — raising all four of their children as observant Jews in the 1930's.

My parents married in 1948 and were childless for the first ten years of their married life. Their joy was boundless when Hashem blessed them with the birth of my sister Dvora (Ostreicher) in 1958, followed by two sons; myself in 1959 and my brother Reb Yehudah in 1961. However, tragedy struck in 1963 when my father *a'h* was suddenly *niftar* at the young age of 41, leaving my mother, *yibodel l'chaim*, with three small children under the age of five.

With the *chesed* of *Hashem* and the unwavering support of her friends and the extended Horowitz/Ganz families, my mother raised us as a single parent for two years until she met and married Reb Shlomo Nutovic in 1965 (who became Abba to the three of us).

Reb Shlomo was born in Arad, Rumania to Reb Baruch Yehuda and Chantza (Appel) Nutovic. During the tumultuous years of World War Two, Reb Baruch Yehudah, his wife and children, Reb Shlomo, Reb Moshe (Bnei Braq and later Williamsburg), and Miriam Waldman (Crown Heights), emigrated to Eretz Yisroel via Bucharest. Reb Shlomo joined the Israeli Army during the War of Independence in 1948, and later moved to Canada, then to New York, where he joined his father Reb Baruch Yehudah *a'h*, in the family jewelry business. There, they both established a reputation for hard work, integrity, and devotion to assisting their extended family members over the years.

Long before the term *blended families* was coined, my parents raised three sets of children as equals (Isaac Nutovic was born to Reb Shlomo from a previous marriage, and my parents were blessed with a child of their own, Chantzie [Rosenberg], a year after they were married) in Belle Harbor, Queens, in an atmosphere of mutual respect, *shalom bayis*, and dignity. Abba graciously and respectfully opened his home to my maternal grandmother, Sara, after she was widowed and she lived near/with us for many years until her *petirah* at the age of ninety. With incredible wisdom, patience, and love, Abba and Mommy raised us and walked all five of their children to the *chuppah*, and with the *chesed* of *Hashem*, are privileged to share in the *simchos* of our children and grandchildren.

This book is dedicated in their honor in recognition of their self-less devotion to their children and of the wonderful example of *emunah*, integrity, resilience, and optimism they have provided to us over the years. May *Hashem* grant them *arichas yomim* and *gezunt*, long life and good health, and may we have the blessing of their inspiration and wisdom for many years to come.

This volume is part of
THE ARTSCROLL SERIES®
an ongoing project of
translations, commentaries and expositions
on Scripture, Mishnah, Talmud, Halachah,
liturgy, history, the classic Rabbinic writings,
biographies and thought.

For a brochure of current publications
visit your local Hebrew bookseller
or contact the publisher:

Mesorah Publications, ltd.

4401 Second Avenue
Brooklyn, New York 11232
(718) 921-9000
www.artscroll.com